Alwyn Crawshaw

THE ARTIST
AT WORK

My Autobiography

HarperCollins*Publishers*

Alwyn Crawshaw
THE ARTIST AT WORK

My Autobiography

First published in 1984 by
William Collins Sons & Co Ltd, London
Reprinted 1985

New edition published in 1996 by
HarperCollins Publishers, London

A catalogue record for this book is available from
the British Library

New edition designed and edited by Flicka Lister
Photography: Nigel Cheffers-Heard

ISBN 0 00 412754 4

Colour origination in Singapore by Colourscan
Produced by HarperCollins Hong Kong

*To June, Natalie, Donna and Clinton
and particularly Mum and Dad*

I would first like to thank all the friends and acquaintances who have helped me along the road to success. I would like to express very special thanks for their unfailing support and encouragement to the late Royston Davies, to my publishers HarperCollins, with particular thanks to Joan Clibbon, Robin Wood and Cathy Gosling, to the staff of Daler-Rowney past and present, to David John Hare, who has produced all my television series, and to John Hope-Hawkins, who has been a tremendous support in recent years and in particular with the Society of Amateur Artists. I would also like to thank the millions of people who read my books and watch my television programmes.

I would also like to express my gratitude to the following for their help in the preparation of this book: Flicka Lister for editing and design, Nigel Cheffers-Heard for the special photography, and Mary Poole for typing the manuscript.

Finally, I owe much to my marriage to June, a partnership that has enriched my painting career and helped to make all the hard work both possible and worthwhile.

CONTENTS

By kind permission of E Stacy-Marks Limited, Eastbourne

FOREWORD

This is the second edition of my autobiography, *The Artist At Work,* which was originally published in 1984. Since that time, I have been involved in a great many exciting activities including the opening of the Crawshaw Gallery and the making of my first television series – which proved to be one of many!

Updating my autobiography has given me the opportunity to include some of my more recent paintings, as well as a few of my favourites. In the first part of the book, which covers my earlier years, some paintings have been added or changed from the original edition. In this new edition, another 32-page section has been added and the book now gives a detailed insight into my painting life up to my sixtieth year.

Alwyn Crawshaw

◀ **Fig. 1** *A Devon Winter,* 41 x 61 cm (16 x 24 in), is an acrylic painting that I worked in the studio. This scene had inspired me when June and I were travelling home from London by car (not the best of journeys in snow like that!). We stopped in a lay-by while I made a quick pencil sketch. More important than the sketch, however, was to engrave on my visual memory the mood of the scene, to give my painting the feeling of open space, distance and, above all, silence

▲ Working at home in my studio at Dawlish in Devon

INTRODUCTION

I am asked so many times: 'How can I become a successful artist?' and my stock answer is: 'You must work hard and have faith in yourself and your work.' That sounds a very grand statement but it is absolutely true. However, in what direction should the hard work be channelled? After all, it is no use having faith in yourself and your work if you are misdirecting your energies.

So I have described many of my experiences in this book in the hope that they will act as guidelines to steer you in the right direction and help you to build a career as an artist, if that is your aim. Bear in mind, however, that there are many different kinds of artists and, therefore, as many different paths that you can take. Mine is just one. For those who are happy painting as a hobby, I hope that you may be encouraged to take further steps forward and learn from the information on techniques used in my paintings here.

I hope that others will be encouraged to take the first step in the direction of painting, and that they will be inspired both by my story and by seeing the progress achieved in my paintings from the very earliest days up to the present. My main aim is to fill every page with practical information and to tell a story that will appeal to anyone, from eight to eighty, who is interested in painting. I want to tell that story now, while I am still a very active artist, painting and selling my work in today's very competitive marketplace, the same marketplace in which any aspiring artist will have to sell his work. I am writing not from the touchline but from the field of play where you have to use your ability and your experience constantly in order to keep ahead.

Another of my aims in writing the book is to answer many of the questions that are so often put to me by the people I meet at exhibitions or while I am lecturing and demonstrating my painting techniques throughout the country. I hope, too, that this book will give an insight into my lifestyle and my work to the people who have read my instructional books and who own my paintings. If it had not been for all these people my artistic career might have been very different.

▶ This page from my photograph album shows me during the early years, from a chubby-cheeked toddler to a young man in his early twenties with his bride-to-be June. In my search for these pictures I was surprised to find some taken of me on painting trips. The one (top left) shows me with one of the first large oil paintings, 51 x 76 cm (20 x 30 in), that I ever did outdoors, when I was just sixteen, and in the one next to it I have Sandy, my ventriloquist's doll, on my knee. The photograph below this was taken before a school cricket match. The one (far top right) was taken during a week's holiday from work, while I was courting June. I spent two days painting an oil of the Basingstoke Canal at Woking, Surrey, and I felt as though I was sitting on a cloud, painting during the day and taking June out in the evenings – what more could a young artist want! The small oval picture shows me in uniform at the beginning of my two years' National Service and below this is 'Alwyno the Crazy Magician' performing during Army days. In the centre is the one all parents love to have – the first school photograph; mine was taken in 1939

SCHOOL-DAYS
1939

ME

K8729

When I have time to sit and think about the past I ask myself what I have acquired most out of my life so far as an artist. I think the most precious acquisition is the ability to see everyday life as a painting. Through painting I have been given the chance to have a second look at nature; to become excited even about a rainy, miserable day and to feel elated by the thought of recreating that mood on paper.

In the introduction to the first edition of this book, written in 1984, I wrote the following words: 'What of the future and where will it take me?'. I then continued: 'Naturally, I don't know but as I love my job I will keep working, experimenting and looking for new subject matter and for new approaches and ideas'. I also added that I would love to travel around the country working on a series of watercolour paintings and writing about my experiences. I wanted to do more oil painting and more pastel painting and was sure that the road ahead was going to be just as full, exciting and rewarding as the journey had been thus far.

Well, more than ten years have passed and I must say I do feel very privileged to be able to continue my story. Naturally, when I wrote the last paragraph, a decade ago, the future seemed a lifetime away. Now that it has come and gone, it has left me with more experience of painting, writing, teaching and life in general as well as some wonderful memories. Of course, I am a little older but I don't feel any different. My brush works over

a canvas just as quickly, and my brain is as active as ever. However, I do find I like to stop a couple of times and look at the view when I am walking up a steep hill nowadays – well, you don't want to miss a good spot for painting!

I have travelled around painting watercolours and written about the experience in books, and I have done more oil painting. But unfortunately I haven't done as much pastel painting as I would have liked.

When I sat down to write about the last ten years, I could have written four or five books on this period alone because it has been such an extremely busy and rewarding time of my life. But, thanks to my editor, I have been kept firmly in control!

I hope you enjoy this book. It takes approximately twelve months after I have finished writing before a book is published and on the bookshelves. Therefore, as you read this, I will be at least one year nearer the third edition and perhaps once again I will have the privilege of bringing you up to date with my working life!

▶ Here is another page from my photograph album which spans many more exciting years for the Crawshaw family. The photograph (top left) was taken in 1957 on the happiest day of my life when June and I became man and wife. The picture next to this shows me with my sister-in-law Dorothy and our firstborn, Natalie, in the summer of 1960. On the right of this, June and I relax on another holiday and next to that I'm shown back at work and obviously in a business mood. (I wonder whatever happened to that black beard?) On the far right is a treasured photograph of my mother with our three children, Donna, Clinton and Natalie, taken in 1973. The photograph (centre row, left) shows young Clinton in 1982 – every bit the budding artist – and next to him

Donna giving her father some sketching tips. To the right of this, June adjusts Natalie's wedding dress on her big day in 1979 while a very proud father of the bride stands by, ready to take orders! Three years later, it was Donna and Andrew's turn to walk down the aisle and give us a wonderful day to remember. The final pictures (from left to right) show June with grandson Russell and newly-arrived granddaughter Heather in 1985. Alongide this are Donna with her two daughters, Poppy and Rebecca, in the summer of 1994. The fishing expedition with Russell that summer resulted in his catching more fish (but did his grandfather let him?). Finally, on the far right, June and I pose for a family photograph with my twin sister Shirley, Natalie and my sister Pam in our Dawlish gallery

◆Chapter 1◆

THE EARLY YEARS

From the age of seven I wanted to be an artist. Today I consider myself very lucky to be doing what I always wanted to do and still getting so much pleasure from it. But how did it all start and what made it work?

First of all, having said how lucky I consider myself to be, I have to confess that I don't really believe that luck, as we accept the word, comes into it. You can't simply sit back and wait for lady luck to smile on you. You have to work hard at your craft and work hard at being in the right place at the right time – and then you may meet lady luck.

I met her when I started as a freelance commercial artist in London shortly after I was married. I spent the first six months travelling around London with my artwork specimens knocking on the doors of over 300 advertising agencies and printers. During that time I placed an advertisement in the *Advertiser's Weekly*; it was four months before I received a reply, from a company called Thames Board Mills Ltd at Purfleet in Essex, asking me to post them samples of my work.

I knew nothing about the company but, determined to get on, I picked up the phone and made an appointment to take some samples to show them that same afternoon. When I arrived, I discovered that the company was one of the largest manufacturers of cardboard packaging in the country. I came away with a test job to do in four days. I did it in two (burning the midnight oil) and so delivered it two days early. They were impressed! I learned later that my advertisement had been found by someone who had pulled out two magazines from a pile of twenty or so, taken three freelance advertisements from each and written to the artists. I happened to be one of those artists.

That day lady luck shone down on me but only after a lot of perseverance. During those first few months I had been getting a little work here and there. At times I had discussed with my wife, June, the awful possibility of calling it a day and getting a full-time job again. We had to live! But I knew what I wanted and I continued to walk the streets of London trying to sell my work.

When I eventually received the letter from Thames Board Mills, the speed with which I

▲ **Fig. 2** This early pencil drawing has survived. It was done when I was ten years old

▼ **Fig. 4** shows a view looking up towards Senlac Hill in Sussex, with Battle Abbey in the far distance. I recall the biggest challenge for me with this picture was painting the mass of green trees. It was while I was working on this painting that I realized more than at any other time the value of observation. I remember how carefully I studied the shapes and colours of the trees and then simplified them in my mind before I started painting them. The distinctive shape and colour of the willows helped to make the trees 'read'

▲ **Fig. 3** This is the picture I was so proudly displaying in the photograph on page 8! It shows a country lane in the spring. I found the area of 'solid' branches between the tree trunks very difficult to paint. I resorted to scratching out some small branches with a palette knife while the paint was wet but I wasn't very pleased with the result. I was happy with the effects I achieved in the path and found that by adding more blue the colours became cooler and I could create the shadow areas. I also learned, particularly when I was painting the gate, how to show shape and form by using light against dark.

I was pleased with the atmosphere of the painting – I felt I had captured the blustery, sunny feeling of spring. The painting was completed on location in one day. Time is not important, however; we all have our natural speed and it doesn't matter if you work fast or slowly

reacted and carried out the work, delivering it two days early, backed up lady luck and I had my first major client. My freelance commercial art career was born. I was twenty-three years old then and much had happened from the age of seven before I reached those dizzy heights!

I was five years old and living in Mirfield, Yorkshire, when the Second World War started. My memories are of sleeping in the garden air-raid shelter, aeroplane spotting and taking part in many other wartime activities, but above all of drawing on the kitchen floor with my twin sister, Shirley. Why is it that children love to draw or paint on the floor rather than on a table? We had a dig-for-victory gardening class at school during which the artistic ones among us were encouraged to draw out of doors instead of gardening.

So, at the tender age of eight, we found ourselves drawing from life. The views we had from the gardens were not easy: buildings, roads, cars and so on. I wish I could see some of those old drawings now, especially as we knew nothing about perspective. At that time my parents bought me my first 'how to draw' book, called *How to Draw Horses*. It was my pride and joy and a close companion during those early years, especially in the air-raid shelter at night. I still have the book and treasure it. My last school report for art before we left Yorkshire gave me 28 out of 30 and an 'excellent' grade.

When I was eleven years old, my family moved to Hastings in Sussex and I went to

▲ **Fig. 5**

14

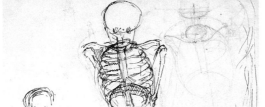

▲ Fig. 6

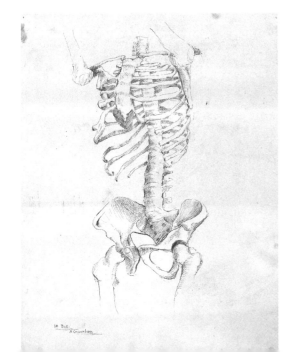

◄ Fig. 7

By courtesy of the *Hastings & St Leonards Observer*

Figs. 5, 6 and **7** are black and white drawings done at school. Life drawing was never my strongest subject, but the exercises taught me to draw, especially bones!

▲ The students from the art school with their float prepare for the Hastings Summer Carnival procession in July 1951. I am fourth from the right (with the beret!) and my twin sister, Shirley, is second from the right

Hastings Grammar School. The school was very academic, which didn't suit me at all. It was also very disciplined – touch your toes and six of the best – in the old, traditional manner. No one liked that side of school life, but when I started out in the world I accepted the discipline as good grounding. The discipline administered both at school and in the Army during my National Service gave me the strength of character to start on my own to become an artist.

One good thing about the grammar school was that it had a very good art class and an excellent art master. Perhaps the signs were there when the headmaster wrote on one year-end report: 'Crawshaw must understand there is more to school than art and sport'. I played football and cricket for my house and junior school teams. That particular year I won the school art prize.

Eventually art won the day. With the blessing of my parents, the headmaster, the art master and the principal of the Hastings School of Art, the late Vincent Lines, I left the grammar school early, at the age of fifteen, and went – with my twin sister – to the art school in Hastings. The next two years were the happiest of my young life.

The thought that I was going to school just to paint was out of this world. Going straight from a very strict academic environment into a casual, sympathetic and creative world was just like a fairy story. But at this point, let me say that at a school like that the amount of effort you put into learning is entirely up to you. You can plod along, jog along or put pressure on yourself and push yourself along. The discipline learnt at the grammar school helped to steer me through art school and keep me firmly on the rails. While I was at art school my family moved to Battle, a town seven miles from Hastings, and we lived in a house on the hill where the Battle of Hastings was fought in 1066. Fig. 4 on page 13 is a painting I did of the hill, with Battle Abbey in the distance.

Figs. 8, 9, 10 and 11 are typical of the watercolour studies we used to do out-of-doors at art school. The object of the exercises was to get us used to working from nature, to teach us to be patient with curious onlookers and, above all, to teach us to observe and simplify. Before I started Fig. 8, I studied the movement of the waves for over half an hour. I then mixed a very watery blue wash and an orange/brown wash and painted in an impression of the breaking waves, using a size 8 sable brush. Back at school, I used this study to paint a finished watercolour (Fig. 9) but it never captured the spirit of the one worked from nature. However, at the time I thought it was a masterpiece! The simple treatment of subject matter and the restricted use of colours in Figs. 10 and 11 (three primary colours plus brown and green) were important in learning watercolour techniques. I used a size 8 round sable brush (I would have been happier using a larger brush if I had been able to afford one) and a size 2 for the small detail work

▲ Fig. 8

▲ Fig. 9   ▼ Fig. 10

▲ Fig. 11

▶ Fig. 12

Figs. 12, **13** and **14** are still life paintings in watercolour which were fundamental to our drawing and painting studies. Everything was under controlled conditions: the lighting, the subject, comfortable working positions, and the tutor on the spot to help at any given time. I vividly remember working on Fig. 13. I painted the fish wet-on-wet (this simply means painting a second colour wash over the first wash while it is still wet) and was very pleased with the result. At the time I was learning how important shadows are to a painting, to help to give shape and form

▶ Fig. 13

▶ Fig. 14

During those art school years I filled every minute of every day and evening painting pictures, drawing and experimenting with different mediums. My relaxation from painting was playing football and cricket for Battle, fishing, conjuring and ventriloquism. Where did I get the energy from? It must have been youth – and the days must have been longer!

I was very fortunate to be in a class of only seven students, which meant that we had a great deal of attention from the tutors, and it was almost like being taught privately. We were taught how to draw and paint in a realistic way, which was not frowned upon as it sometimes is today. The reasoning behind this seems very obvious and basic to me. You must learn your craft from the bottom until you can master it – and only then are you capable of experimenting with it. I was always taught that technique can be learnt. Take, for example, dry brush technique. This is done in the same way by all artists, but each one shows a personal touch. This is style, which, given time, will emerge and show itself, and will make every artist's work different.

My first report from the principal read: 'He has worked very well with marked ability in drawing. He has made progress and has shown definite promise'. This report certainly inspired me for the following year!

Each term at art school the principal gave a prize for the best painting done during the term. In my second year, I won the coveted prize. I was so proud and, at sixteen, it looked as if I was still on the

▲ Fig. 15

▶ Fig. 16

Figs. 15 and 16 were both painted with watercolour mixed with white gouache, which turns the transparent colours opaque. It is a way of painting that any student should experiment with.
Fig. 15 shows my local church in the old town of Hastings, which I painted on the spot. I was a choirboy there and I have many happy memories of this church. The object of the study – apart from developing drawing skills – was to create the feeling of strength and solidity, which is quite different from the previous exercises of painting crashing waves or blowing trees.
Fig. 16 shows a typical 'draped life' study; the exercise was to paint whoever was in front of us as we sat at our desks or easels

tracks to becoming an artist. The painting is illustrated in Fig. 17 (below), and I still have it in my studio.

Sadly, the two years at art school had to end when my family moved to Woking in Surrey. There I started to look for work and, eventually, I was fortunate enough – I was one of forty-eight applicants – to get a job as a trainee commercial artist at a firm in London which published magazines for the engineering, pharmaceutical and ironmongery trades. I had an excellent grounding there, learning the disciplines of graphic design, hand-drawn lettering, black and white and colour illustration, airbrushing, paste-up, and many other aspects of general commercial art. As usual I worked very hard (I'm the type of person that always has to be doing something – mind you, I find that now there are times when I weaken and do nothing!) and in the evenings at home I carried on painting pictures.

Once a month – on the Saturday following payday – I would catch a train to London and spend some of my money at a conjuring trick shop, buying new tricks. I now did conjuring and ventriloquism semi-professionally under the name of 'Alwyno the Crazy Magician' – those were the days! I would then go along to the Constable room at the National Gallery and gaze at his paintings in awe, unaware of anyone else in the room. I was brought up on John Constable at art school; he was my number one artist and he still is. However, over the years he has had to share the stage with some of the French Impressionists, whom I have come to admire more and more, together with some of our contemporary artists. But it is the influence of Constable's work that played such a great part in my love of landscape and in the choice of it as my painting subject. Perhaps the one feature of his work that has inspired me more than any other is his skies; they have so much depth and distance and convey such feelings of space and light.

In the early 1970s June and I went on a painting pilgrimage to Constable Country, staying near his birthplace at East Bergholt,

◀ **Fig. 17** This won me the coveted prize at art school. I painted it in oils on paper and particularly like the all-over blue and grey colour. But look at the coat draped over the chairback – it's hanging on nothing. Learn to observe, young Alwyn!

A small selection of merchandising material which has been designed and progressed to finished artwork stage by Russell Artists Merchandising Limited

What a change from art school work! **Figs. 18** and **19** are pages from two of the promotional leaflets we produced at Russell Artists to demonstrate the type of work in which we were involved. The work was exciting but very severe on artistic precision. A good design sense, complete accuracy, a small sable brush and spotlessly clean work were essential. It was artistic discipline at its keenest

◀ Fig. 18

▲ Fig. 19

Suffolk. What a fabulous week that was. I explored the area thoroughly and worked relentlessly, almost as if someone was going to take it all away from me. I still refer to some of the sketches and other work undertaken during that time.

Constable's influence on me and my work is undoubtedly profound, so I find it puzzling that, whereas most of his landscapes are summer scenes with trees in full leaf, most of mine show a time of year when the trees have lost their leaves. Nevertheless, each season holds its own magic for me. When I am out working in the spring I feel as if I want to paint it forever and no other season could inspire me again. Yet when the spring turns to summer and the small leaves lose their bright green hues – and I find myself using more Yellow Ochre and Crimson – I get deeply involved and I am not concerned about the spring any more. I react in the same way to all the seasons; when one dies I am ready for the next. Naturally, I can paint a picture out of season in the studio but there are times when the seasonal characteristics are so strong that I can only paint a picture capturing the outside elements of that day.

Each Saturday, during my first year as a trainee commercial artist, just before I left the National Gallery to catch my train home,

◀ **Fig. 20** shows, on the left, one of the first Surf packs to carry a promotion. I designed this at home on the kitchen table one weekend in the early 1960s. For the Lux toilet soap window sticker on the right, I used gouache (an opaque watercolour) and worked with an airbrush, then lettered the wording over the top with a paintbrush

▶ **Fig. 21**

I would have a long last look at a certain part of a Constable painting and memorize it, and then I would try to emulate it in the evening. I missed only one or two monthly Saturday trips to London during that time, and then the Army took over for two years.

I didn't do much painting while I was in the Army at Aldershot, but I enjoyed the cricket, football and the comradeship. Although I didn't appreciate it at the time, the discipline helped me tremendously in later years. I had some great times and made some very good friends. Thirty-nine years later, I met Lofty, one of my best friends from the Army, at one of my road shows!

After two years I was demobbed and returned to my old job. I carried on training and working hard for another eighteen months and then I married June. Three months later I went freelance. After the precarious beginning that I related earlier, I became established as a freelance artist, and

The illustrations in **Figs. 21** and **22** are relatively free in style compared to some commercial illustration work. I used gouache for the aeroplane and watercolour for the car

◀ **Fig. 22**

after a couple of years Bill Showell, a very great friend of mine, joined me in partnership and we established a company called Russell Artists in Russell Square, London.

This partnership was to continue for twenty-two very happy years, until I eventually resigned from the company in 1980, having been through the hectic boom times of the 1960s and the pop art scene to the recession times of the late 1970s. I had been planning to leave the company since 1968 when I started a slow retreat from commercial art into fine art painting. During those years, I was helping to run the company at the same time as painting at home and promoting myself. It was very time-consuming but rewarding.

The business experience I gained during my commercial art era – employing staff, promoting the studio, running accounts, winning new clients and dealing with creative people, brand managers and marketing managers of national and international companies – played a tremendous part in equipping me with the ability to sell myself and then my paintings to agents, galleries, private individuals, fine art print publishers, colour manufacturers, and so on.

The painting experience of commercial art helped to train me to draw, design, illustrate, to be creative, to observe and to give me many more of the attributes that an artist needs. People have said to me: 'Where would you be now if you had painted during those years instead of going into commercial art?'

◄ In this photograph, June and I are standing in front of my work during the annual spring Thames Embankment painting exhibition in London in the early 1960s. It lasted a week and was fairly cold but very enjoyable

► **Fig. 23** is a watercolour, 25 x 38 cm (10 x 15 in), of the Basingstoke Canal. I painted it one evening in 1956 after work and June is the model on the bridge. I'm not sure whether the bridge is leaning to the right – I think it may be!

Naturally, I can't answer that, but I sincerely believe that all those years gave me an invaluable training. Without it I might not have succeeded at all. One vital thing that it did do was enable me, after leaving art school, to carry on using a pencil and brush and to earn a living from drawing and painting. For that alone I am forever grateful for the commercial art years of my life and to the many, many friends who helped me.

Wet and Windy

Listen to radio or television weather forecasts and I guarantee you'll frequently hear the words 'wet and windy'. Every time I hear them I get a shiver down my spine, for that was the title given to my first successful fine art print.

The painting was inspired by a visit to a heavy horse ploughing match. Since the day, in my early childhood, when I was given my *How to Draw Horses* book, I had been fascinated by these lovely animals but I had never given them serious consideration as subject matter for my paintings. Now, forty years on, as I watched the heavy horses at work I was filled with enthusiasm and inspiration.

I made enquiries on the whereabouts of any local heavy horses and was delighted to learn that a nursery nearby used two of them on the land. I obtained permission to sketch the horses, and then I started to paint them in my pictures. *Wet and Windy* was, in fact, the third 'horse' painting I did and I took it along, together with three other paintings, to my publisher, Felix Rosenstiel's. It was chosen for publication. It was an immediate

Black tyre

Wet and Windy grew and matured; it was not a spontaneous creation. I doodled with my pencil trying to design a picture that would combine horses and landscape – these are some of the thumbnail sketches that I made. At one stage I was going to have two grey horses against a stormy dark sky (top right). I experimented with a powerful sketch of horses almost stepping out of the picture (centre far right). I actually used this sketch for an acrylic painting and presented it with *Wet and Windy* to the print publishers for consideration, but it was felt that the horses were too overpowering. The thumbnail sketch (above right) is the nearest to the finished painting, with dark horses against a light sky. This sketch suggests two groups of trees on the right, but I used only one in the finished painting; at that point I hadn't thought of including a fire. The fire was put in when the painting was nearing completion

Dark horses
Light sky

Very Dark Sky
grey horses

Sunset
orange
yellow

very light

◀ My final sketch for *Wet and Windy* (left) was drawn on layout paper; in those days I did most of my preliminary work on that type of paper. The sketch is 25 x 51cm (10 x 20 in), half the size of the finished painting on page 26. I took out the second group of trees to simplify the picture and to show more sky, giving a feeling of space and freedom

success and was sold all over the world. In 1975, when the print was in its second year, it was included among the top ten prints chosen by the members of the Fine Art Trade Guild.

On the day of the announcement all ten prints were shown on BBC television's *Nationwide*. It was a strange feeling as I sat with my family watching the programme, especially when the picture was shown in close-up and filled the screen.

Following its success, I received a flood of requests from gallery owners for paintings of heavy horses and elm trees (my favourite trees). I became known for this particular subject matter and even now the accepted 'Crawshaw painting' is one depicting working horses and elm trees. Naturally I enjoy the popularity of this type of painting but I also like to express myself in many other, different ways, using a great variety of subjects.

My first BBC radio appearance followed shortly after the print had been shown on television. I was contacted by the producer of a programme called *Jack de Manio Precisely*, who wanted me to be interviewed. The recording took place at Broadcasting House in London and was planned for broadcast the following week.

On the day of the broadcast June and I had gone to Cambridge for a meeting to discuss and organize a week's painting demonstration I was to undertake the following month. We travelled home in the afternoon and just before the programme was due to start I stopped the car in a lay-by. With the windows closed tight to deaden the traffic noise June and I listened intently to my first radio broadcast. What an exciting moment that was!

▶ **Fig. 24** shows the finished acrylic painting, 51 x 101 cm (20 x 40 in). I started, as usual, by painting the sky, then worked in the distance up to the near field. The next stage was to paint the distant trees and then the largest tree. Once I had established the background and middle distance, I settled down to work on the horses (without detail at this stage) and then the logs. The foreground was a bit awesome – that huge expanse of blank canvas – but I had decided to make it quite free. I used a size 8 flat nylon brush and as I worked I added texture paste to the paint (this is an acrylic medium of thick paste consistency), to help create the texture of mud and earth. The whole canvas was now covered, and this was the time to study and reflect. It was at this stage that I decided to add the fire, the man feeding it and the waiting horse near the large tree. Looking at the painting now after years of hard-earned experience, I could find numerous faults. For instance, I'm sure the logs are too round and regular and – had anyone noticed? – I didn't paint in the right-hand blinker on the right-hand horse! But then it's a painting, not a technical drawing, and *Wet and Windy* will stay close to my heart as long as I live

◆Chapter 2◆

A STYLE OF MY OWN

In 1968 I found I was beginning to get very restless with work. Things were running smoothly with the commercial art company and I had time on my hands. 'Why don't you start painting pictures again?' said June one day. I'm sure now that, apart from when June agreed to marry me, this question brought about the greatest change in our lives. The incredible thing was that it had to be asked at all of someone who, even at the age of seven, knew he wanted to become an artist.

What had happened to this man? In retrospect, the answer was simple. I had given my whole self to commercial art since leaving art school and it needed someone to see when I was ready to be steered more directly onto my chosen path. June had sensed this and asked the question at exactly the right time. Was this luck again, or a clever wife? Within minutes my brain was working overtime. 'You know what it'll mean?' I said. 'I'll put everything I have into it and I'll be back to working seven days a week, and evenings as well.' 'Off you go,' said June, and another phase of my painting career was born.

▶ **Fig. 25** Airbrush paintings are to be seen today far more than in the early 1960s when I airbrushed my way through this aeroplane. It is a very exacting way of working and I prefer the freedom of the paint brush, but the experience I gained is part of my artistic make-up

My hardest task was to 'loosen up' my painting, to retrain my eye and mind not to look directly for detail and definition, which, in commercial art, are the prime considerations. Figs. 26 and 27 (opposite) are examples of my 'natural' work. The common rules of painting are the same but the application is totally different. That was 1968, and, since then, 'super realism', a style of painting that looks even more real than a photograph, has emerged. The trained eye of a commercial artist helps to achieve this style of painting, and some artists use the airbrush, a very fine spray gun, to obtain some of the effects. The airbrush started as a commercial art tool for retouching photographs or for illustrating to represent photographs. Fig. 25 (above) shows one of the very first airbrush drawings that I did for commercial art in the early 1960s.

▲ **Fig. 26** *Melting Snow*, 41 x 30 cm (16 x 12 in), was worked in acrylic colours on canvas. I started by covering the whole canvas with varying mixtures of Coeruleum Blue, Crimson, Cadmium Yellow and White. When the background was dry I painted in the trees and hedges. At that point the foreground was flat and featureless, so I worked over it with thicker paint and added some detail feature lines in the snow for ruts and shadows, to help show the contours. The small, feathery branches on the trees in both paintings were worked with a dry brush technique

Private collection

▲ **Fig. 27** *Going Home*, 41 x 30 cm (16 x 12 in), was painted from memory after a late afternoon walk. The inspiration came from the delicate pastel colouring of the sky, which I achieved in the painting by using Coeruleum Blue, Crimson, Cadmium Yellow and White. I painted the tree in silhouette to help give brightness to the sky and contrast to the picture. Working on winter trees gives me tremendous pleasure; I can get lost for hours painting their branches

I started by using oil colours and I worked hard at 'seeing' painting in a different way. Although I had painted in oils since leaving art school, I was now painting for long hours and so my work and my mind had to change. Because of my need for putting in detail (I knew I had to change my approach but I like detail in a painting), I was finding that the long drying time oils require was restricting me.

Some artists who work in oils may have up to three or more paintings on the go at the same time, but I find this very difficult. When I get inspiration to start a painting, all my senses are directed to the mood I want to convey to the painting and subsequently to the onlooker. A painting must say something; it is a statement in paint. That 'something' can be anything from an action to a simple interpretation of a tree by a river but, above all else, the painting must have a mood, an atmosphere that one can relate to. To maintain the mood I find I must constantly keep painting that one picture. Detail work and finishing touches can be added at almost any time, but the 'meat' of the painting, enough to convey the mood, has to be done in one sitting.

For instance, when I am painting a sky, I cannot be interrupted. Unless the home were burning down nothing would get me from my easel. I believe the sky sets the mood of the painting; it tells us if it is warm, cold, windy, raining, misty or snowing, and it must have my undivided attention.

Having recognized the restrictions oils presented to me in their long drying time, I was most interested by the introduction, in 1969, of artists' quality acrylic colour. I was told it dried almost immediately, and although at first I didn't like the look of it in its see-through plastic tubes, I eventually decided to use some to block in the background to an oil painting. If it really was so quick drying I could work over the top in oils and so save a lot of time. It is at the beginning of a painting when I need to progress as fast as my inspiration and ability will allow. The method worked and I was delighted. For the next painting I went a little further with the acrylic colour and by the sixth painting I was doing two-thirds of it using acrylic colours. I then realized that I had stumbled on a painting medium that was to help establish my career as a painter — lady luck had struck again.

There was only one problem with acrylic colours. Being a new medium at that time, there was no-one to turn to for practical advice for painting techniques or painting methods, nor were there any books available on the subject. Now here was a challenge that would keep me busy. Using all my watercolour and oil painting knowledge, together with technical help from Rowney (I used their colours), I found myself on the road to painting the type of pictures I wanted to paint, using a medium that I felt, once mastered, was all I could ask for. However, it was very difficult being a pioneer, using a medium that was not established and that art

galleries were wary of. Here I was, an unknown artist in a new world, trying to sell pictures painted in a brand new medium.

The same hopeless feeling that I had had at the beginning of my commercial art days crept in and I wondered whether to give up trying with acrylics and go back to oils. But I kept reasoning that I was unknown, that I needed as much help as possible to become known, so what better way than by being referred to as 'the artist who uses that new painting medium – acrylic colour'? In fact, six years later when I did my first BBC radio broadcast on *Jack de Manio Precisely*, I was introduced as 'an artist who is making quite a name for himself painting with plastic paints'. I was horrified when I heard it. I felt like a freak who had discovered gimmicky colours to paint and sell gimmicky paintings, but after the initial shock waves had subsided, I accepted it as good publicity. I was becoming known as the artist who worked in acrylic colours.

One of the most worrying thoughts that concerned me at art school was the fear of not being able to develop a style of my own. When I was painting in oils I was emulating, to a certain extent, Constable's paintings. With my watercolour paintings (most of them are painted outside on location) I have always painted what I see and have never worried about my own watercolour style, as I feel it has always been 'me'. But my style of oil painting worried me. That worry dissolved when I started with acrylic colours. I found my own

Author's collection

◀ **Fig. 28** *Austin's Crow,* 76 x 51cm (30 x 20 in), is a watercolour I painted as a challenge. Austin, a family friend who does taxidermy as a hobby, gave me a stuffed crow and I decided to try painting it. I made a setting for the bird with a log and some ivy on a piece of hardboard covered with earth and stones. The challenge was threefold: I had never painted a crow before; I was going to paint it a large size; and I had decided that I was not to use any white paint, so I would have to leave areas of unpainted white paper for all the highlights. I drew the bird and log on Whatman paper, which I soaked with water with my brush, taking care not to wet the area of the bird. I then laid in a warm grey wash, again covering all the areas except the bird. I built wash on wash with sizes 10 and 6 round sable brushes, guarding against too much colour in the areas I wanted to be light. The main colours used for the crow were French Ultramarine, Payne's Grey, Crimson Alizarin and Yellow Ochre. I was pleased with the finished painting as I achieved the result I had aimed for, which is not always possible with watercolour

natural style evolved, through experience, but also by using a totally new medium.

I can split my type of painting into three categories. The first is what I call my 'natural' work, the type of painting I can sit down at the easel with and get completely lost in. If I am in a depressed mood I can start a painting and work my way out of the mood, using the painting as therapy. This type of painting is shown in Figs. 26 and 27 on page 29. There

is very little drawing involved and this gives me more time to concentrate on the painting. I can also 'live' an intimate part of landscape and create it as I paint – even from memory. This has come from years of training myself to observe when I am out on location. Familiarity of my subject matter also helps me with this type of painting. But I never paint these subjects simply to achieve a finished product. Every painting I do is different from start to

▶ **Fig. 29** *The Harbour at Le Val André*, 76 x 152 cm (30 x 60 in), was a challenge in terms of size and subject. It was painted in acrylics on canvas and it was only the second time I had worked at this size. I made some sketches of the harbour in Brittany and took some photographs for boat details, then painted the picture at home in my studio. My biggest problem was starting it! I was terrified at the prospect of painting such a large expanse of water. After doing a war dance round it all morning, I plucked up courage and painted in the sky and water, using Coeruleum Blue, Crimson, Cadmium Yellow and White as my base colours. Once these areas had been established I didn't have any other problems. The feeling of depth was helped enormously by having the quay wall running from the foreground into the distance

Private collection, USA

finish, either in my mind or on the canvas. I never get bored or over-confident. Each one is still a challenge in its own right.

My second type of painting is the one I really have to work at, the one that challenges my observation and drawing as well as my painting skills. Figs. 28 and 29 on pages 31 and 32 are good examples. After painting my 'natural' paintings for a few weeks, I need to involve myself in this type of work to bring me back to earth and 'keep my eye in'. These paintings are good for my morale because they are usually completely different from my normal work and they provide a challenge which keeps my skills sharpened.

The third type of painting is a watercolour worked on location. Figs. 30 and 31 are examples. When I find a subject that inspires me, whether it's in the countryside, the town or by the sea, and I get settled and ready to start, it's like being in heaven! The thrill of capturing the scene in front of me in watercolour is enormous. Even when I am outside in winter and it's freezing cold I enjoy every minute of it. I also use watercolour paintings to provide information for larger acrylic and oil paintings worked in the studio.

As well as these three basic types of work, I paint watercolours and oils in the studio (see Figs. 32 and 33 on pages 36 and 37) and oil paintings and pencil sketches out-of-doors. I get a great deal of pleasure from pencil sketching. Like watercolours done

Author's collection

▲ **Fig. 30**, 38 x 51 cm (15 x 20 in), was painted on the beach at Sidmouth in Devon during a family day out in the hot summer of 1983. I worked on Whatman paper and took my time to draw in plenty of detail first. Before I started painting I studied the scene, thinking about how I would approach it. The most important decision I made was to leave the white paper unpainted for the buildings on the promenade. I worked over the rest of the paper with washes of colour, gradually building them up as I worked more detail into the picture

▶ **Fig. 31**, 28 x 38 cm (11 x 15 in), was painted on Dartmoor, at Post Bridge. The house was the whitest and brightest part of the scene, so I left the paper unpainted in this area. When I had finished the painting some Dartmoor ponies came onto the scene and I was persuaded by June and my sister Pam to put them in the painting. That was a mistake. They should have been planned in at the drawing stage as an integral part of the picture. The result is that they look like a cross between a pony and a cow. However, I was pleased with the picture as it captured the atmosphere of the day

out-of-doors, pencil sketches are a direct and unlaboured statement of what is in front of me (see Figs. 36 and 37 on pages 38 and 39). Finally, I always try to find time to experiment, to try something different, as this keeps me on my toes.

I have always believed that you can only learn to paint and improve your painting by copying nature. Simply, this means that when you are painting landscapes you must paint in the field. However, now, after years of experience and evolving a natural way of working, I see the rôle of painting out-of-doors slightly differently. The value of working outside is immeasurable for gathering information and training the eye to see scale, colours, perspective and so on, but it can sometimes limit the artist's creative ability, as he is copying something already created by nature. Creativity comes from having seen and learnt about the real thing and then creating your own version. A painting created out of an artist's mind's eye can be more fluent and unlaboured than one painted on location. This is because the artist is not concerned with the elements and distractions that are to be found in the field, but only with his own thoughts. He is in a world of his own. But take heed – this way of painting can achieve good results only if the

Private collection

◄ **Fig. 32** *Cows at Metcombe*, 28 x 38 cm (11 x 15 in), was painted in the studio in watercolour from pencil sketches done outside. The cows were painted wet-on-wet technique; notice how I left white paper to show through on some of the cows and, in particular, on the right-hand cow. The colours used were Coeruleum Blue, Payne's Grey, Hooker's Green No. I, Crimson Alizarin and Yellow Ochre, and Cadmium Red for the boy's jumper. The detail was put in when the washes were dry

Fig. 33 *Dell Quay*, 50 x 75 cm (20 x 30 in), was done in oil on canvas from a pencil sketch I did on the spot. I feel the picture has captured 'light' and I painted it very thinly in cool colours. I find that now my paintings have warmed up considerably

Fig. 34 *Copper Trees*, 38 x 50 cm (15 x 20 in), was a watercolour done in my studio. I painted the yellow sun and sky first with a very watery wash. I continued to the bottom of the painting, changing the colours as I went to establish the evening light

Fig. 35 *Evening, Exmouth*, 50 x 75 cm (20 x 30 in), is another estuary scene painted in oil from a pencil sketch. Notice how I put highlights on the fishing boat and the rowing boat to help give them dimension

 ▶ Fig. 34

 ▲ Fig. 33

▲ Fig. 35

Figs. 33–35 are in private collections

artist has worked and studied sufficiently in the field with nature. And even then, he must keep returning to nature for inspiration.

When I am painting in the studio I have a routine, which is most important. The temptations when you are working on your own at home are enormous, and it would be so easy to find distractions. I normally start painting in the morning at around 9.30 and I don't like to embark on an acrylic or oil painting later than about eleven o'clock. If it gets later than that I do office work or I varnish pictures, prime canvases, contact galleries, write articles, answer letters and so on.

Alternatively, I may do some watercolour painting, as the preparation is fairly simple and a small freestyle watercolour can be executed in a very short time.

I work hard during the day and continue up to any event that may be happening in the evening. With all my other activities of writing, teaching, demonstrating, lecturing, opening art society exhibitions, attending various committee meetings, judging art competitions and helping to run a home, I feel very pleased if I have three or four consecutive days for painting pictures. Still, I am never bored!

▲ **Fig. 36**, 23 x 29 cm (9 x 11½ in), is a drawing I did in Soest, West Germany, the town in which June and I stayed during my exhibition in 1982. The figures on these two pages are examples of the type of pencil sketches I love to do when I am in a new venue, or when I want to record something that is different from usual. Both drawings were done with a 2B pencil on cartridge drawing paper

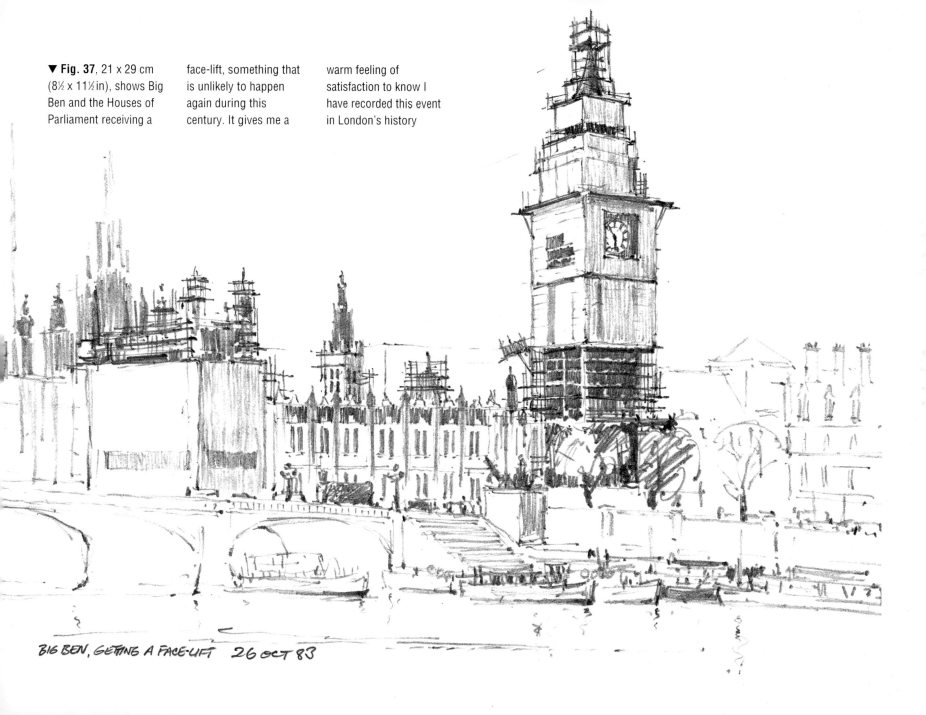

▼ **Fig. 37**, 21 x 29 cm (8½ x 11½ in), shows Big Ben and the Houses of Parliament receiving a face-lift, something that is unlikely to happen again during this century. It gives me a warm feeling of satisfaction to know I have recorded this event in London's history

BIG BEN, GETTING A FACE-LIFT 26 OCT 83

A Day at the Races

I don't think fish and chips will ever taste the same as they did at 8.30 on the morning of the 200th Epsom Derby in 1979. It was my first visit to a race meeting and the media were suggesting that up to half a million people would be attending. What an initiation – and I was going to paint the scene!

I had put a lot of time and effort into planning the painting. On the Saturday prior to the Wednesday meeting I went with a friend who was familiar with the course to find a painting spot and do some preliminary work. I was surprised to find so much going on: the large fairground was in full swing and there were rows of caravans with gipsy fortune-tellers waiting for their palms to be crossed, in return, maybe, for the name of the Derby winner! It was tempting to find out, but I had only one thought in mind: to find the right spot to work from.

We walked through the tunnel under the track near the grandstand and out onto the middle of the course, then up the hill, looking back at the view. I stopped to do two pencil sketches of the stand area. These were very important as the stand and the area around it

would be partly obscured by people on the day. Fig. 38 (opposite) shows one of these sketches, which was done on cartridge paper. We carried on walking up the hill and eventually found the perfect spot at the top. Not only could I see for miles around into the distant countryside, I could also get most of the finishing straight and the stands into the picture. I sat down and worked on another pencil sketch of the view I would paint on the following Wednesday.

At seven o'clock on Derby Day morning, I set off with my daughter Donna, having checked and re-checked the painting equipment to make sure nothing was forgotten. Donna came with me because June wasn't well that day and also because she wanted to do some sketching. By 8.30 a.m. we were parked in precisely the spot I had planned. We then walked down the hill into the rows of stalls selling everything from sweets and teddy bears to wall mirrors, brass

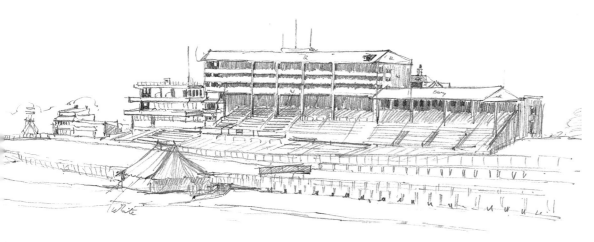

◀ **Fig. 38** is one of the sketches, 28 x 41 cm (11 x 16 in), of the main stand area that I made on the Saturday prior to the race meeting

Author's collection

◀ **Fig. 39** is the watercolour, 37 x 53 cm (14½ x 21 in), I painted on the day. During the four hours I was drawing and painting, the scene was constantly changing in front of me as more coaches and cars converged on the meeting. I coped with the situation by first drawing the parts of the scene that would not change – the stands, marquees, trees – then putting in the foreground, with the coaches, cars and so on. At that point I decided I would paint exactly what I had drawn. If, however, some interesting shapes and colours were formed by more arrivals while I was painting the sky and stand area I would draw them in before I started to paint the foreground. Once I had started painting the foreground I had to paint what was drawn. A watercolour has to be planned and because of the way the colours have to be applied, working light to dark, you must follow your plan. When I had finished the picture there was a lot more activity than my painting shows

ornaments and T-shirts and had a second breakfast of delicious fish and chips.

We wandered around absorbing the atmosphere – for me it was not so much a day at the races (they seemed so far away, in the afternoon), it was an experience of life, anticipation and excitement.

The urge to start painting eventually took over, so we walked up the hill to my vantage point. I got settled down with my drawing board, paper and watercolour paints and just sat and looked at the scene for about half an hour to familiarize myself with it. I then started and worked solidly for a couple of hours, before taking a short break and continuing for a further two hours.

Because of the sketching I had done on the previous Saturday I felt at ease working; the scene was familiar and this helped me to concentrate on the colour and atmosphere of the painting.

I used a size 10 round sable brush for the large area washes and a size 6 for the detail work. I included the two solitary figures to show scale and distance (see Fig. 39 on the previous page).

Once the watercolour was completed I relaxed and did some general sketching, backed the loser of the Derby and finally got home at about eight o'clock. I was exhausted but very pleased with the day's work.

I had plenty of sketches, a watercolour of the scene and I had also taken some photographs for reference. The plan was to paint a large picture in acrylic colours, so

with all my information I started one morning in the studio and worked on a canvas measuring 76 x 152 cm (30 x 60 in). The finished result is shown in Fig. 40.

To paint a picture of this size and complexity you must have a great deal of information and first-hand experience of the occasion. I found it a tremendous challenge from the first pencil sketch to the last brush stroke on the large canvas.

▶ **Fig. 40** shows the finished acrylic painting, 76 x 152 cm (30 x 60 in). I started by painting the sky and distant countryside behind the stand and dark trees, then I blocked in the painting using thin paint. This established the distance to my foreground, tonally, and it also gave me a colour to work on for the detail in the stand and foreground. I painted over the people in the stand three times before I was satisfied that they stayed in the stand and did not jump out of the picture! Notice how little real detail there is in the coaches and cars except

for the four main coaches running across the picture. As the painting had to be worked on as a whole I guarded against getting too involved with a particular detail area; this can be very difficult and needs a lot of discipline. The painting took about a week to complete but I had it in the studio for a further few weeks, during which time I made adjustments here and there. Upon reflection, I wish I had made the stand larger to give a little more drama to the picture

Private collection

42

By kind permission of the Salston Hotel, Devon

Chapter 3

ON SHOW

The title of this chapter sums up an artist's life very well. If an artist is to climb the ladder of success he and his work must be on show as much as possible.

When my first paintings were admired by my family and friends it gave me tremendous inspiration to keep working. I gave paintings away to admirers and they went from my studio to their lounge walls. There they would be seen by friends and visitors, some of whom would buy a painting from me and so another one would travel direct from studio to lounge wall.

I'm sure most artists have started their career by parting with their pictures in this way. However, it is a very slow method and if you are a prolific artist you will soon find your loft full of paintings. The far bigger drawback is that the public will not be seeing your paintings and therefore won't know of your existence. But how do you get your work into the public eye?

I knew I had to channel the feelings of challenge and excitement I had at that time into something practical and positive. I decided to contact some friends who ran a

local restaurant, to see if they would display some of my work – they agreed. Throughout my life, whatever I have involved myself in I have always given it my complete enthusiasm and energy. Therefore, painting pictures for that restaurant was as exciting and as important to me then as staging a

▶ **Fig. 41** *Early Spring, Itchenor, Sussex,* 41 x 51 cm (16 x 20 in), was painted in acrylic colours from the pencil sketch (shown above), during the time we had a house at nearby Bracklesham Bay. The painting was hung at my exhibition at the Solomon and Whitehead gallery in London in 1975

By kind permission of Mr and Mrs W. Showell

Private collection

◀ **Fig. 42** is a detail from an acrylic painting, 51 x 101 cm (20 x 40 in). I can still remember the smell of the steam-powered farm machines from the days when, as a boy, I used to play in the corn stooks with my childhood friends. I was delighted a few years ago to rediscover some old threshing machines on a visit to a country fair in Surrey. I painted a watercolour of the scene and used it for an acrylic painting. I used Raw Sienna as the main colour for the wheat, adding a little Cadmium Yellow, Crimson, Raw Umber and White. For the dark shadow areas I added a little Ultramarine Blue. The painting was hung in a mixed artists' exhibition at the John Birch Fine Art Gallery in Croydon, Surrey. John has given me great encouragement over the years, and he organized my first Harrods exhibition

▶ **Fig. 43** *And The Rains Never Came*, 51 x 76 cm (20 x 30 in), was painted in acrylics for the 1981 Harrods exhibition. I was trying to convey the type of threatening sky that sometimes comes over in the summer, bringing with it a feeling of eeriness and unreality. It plunges the landscape into darkness, yet the sun remains out in some areas; a downpour seems certain, but it never comes. The main colour used for the sky was Coeruleum Blue mixed with Cadmium Yellow and Crimson, and there are touches of Raw Umber and White in some places. For the cornfield I used mainly Cadmium Yellow, Crimson, Raw Umber and White. Many people at the exhibition thought the painting was overpowering, but someone fell in love with it and bought it

one-man exhibition in a top class gallery is now. The paintings were completed, framed and hung in the restaurant. Two weeks later the first picture was sold. What a thrill it was that a total stranger had paid money for something I had created, because he wanted to have it in his home to get pleasure from it. At that point, all the hard work so far had been worthwhile.

About eighteen months and hundreds of painting hours later, in the spring of 1970, I had my first one-man show in our local stationer's and art supplier's shop, which was managed by a friend of mine, Tim Aldridge. He suggested the idea of the show to me and

so I painted about twenty-eight pictures for it. The paintings were hung everywhere in the shop – over the pen counter, the greetings cards counter, in the book department area and in every space a painting could be hung. June and I were there on the first day of the exhibition, feeling rather nervous but excited. Some paintings were sold that day and by the end of the show two weeks later only three were left. One of the paintings sold, *First Breath of Spring*, was later reproduced as a fine art print (see Fig. 48 on page 53).

During this time I was constantly taking pictures around to galleries to see if they were

Private collection

Private collection

▲ **Fig. 44** *From St. Catherine's, Guildford*, 38 x 50 cm (15 x 20 in). Most of my watercolours of that era (1975–80) were heavier in colour than those I do today. Fig. 111 on page 118, which was also done outside, is much lighter. This hasn't happened consciously – it is a natural evolution, just as my paintings have got 'warmer' over the years. I must say I like the strength of this painting, although I also like the delicacy of my later watercolours. I suppose, as long as you like what you're doing, you should let evolution take its course!

interested in buying them (usually on a sale or return basis). It was quite a problem doing the two jobs at once – painting and selling.

Eventually, Felix Rosenstiel's, the publishers of my first print, agreed to take my paintings and sell them for me to galleries. This arrangement brought about some important changes. I now had much more time for painting (always my number one commitment), my work was being handled by professionals, but I was earning much less per painting as the publishers were taking a percentage of the selling price. However, I've always accepted the price you have to pay for an agent's work.

In the next two years or so my paintings were seen in many well-known galleries all over the country. I know I could never have achieved this on my own but I also attribute my having reached this position so relatively quickly to long hours and hard work. Like any job, painting is work and if you are to make any headway you simply have to work very hard not only at your painting but at selling, which helps you to become known, which, in turn, helps to sell your paintings... So my strong advice to aspiring artists of any age is: paint, paint and paint (I try to do a painting or pencil sketch a day), and when you're not painting, go out and sell your work. Apart from a very few exceptions, agree to your work being hung anywhere. Remember, a painting leaving your studio direct to a lounge wall will not get you known. Your work must always be on show.

My first important one-man show was held in October 1973 at the Barclay Art Gallery in Chester, to which I was introduced by Eddy Vernon, who handled the sales of my paintings. Once the introduction was made, I was left to arrange the exhibition direct with the gallery owner. I couldn't have had a better start for my first major one-man show. The exhibition was given plenty of publicity, with reports in the important northwest newspapers and county magazines, and the Duchess of Westminster agreed to open the exhibition. The first night was an enormous success, an evening June and I will never forget. The evening was further enhanced when June and I, together with our two daughters, Natalie and Donna, were invited by the Duchess to tea two days later at Eaton Hall, her home in Chester. After tea, the Duchess showed us her art treasures – a fantastic collection we could have looked at forever.

This event was followed by a hectic period of painting for galleries that wanted more of my work. Then came a tremendous breakthrough: Harrods, the world-famous department store in Knightsbridge, London, invited me to put on an exhibition in their art gallery at the end of 1974. While I was preparing for the Harrods exhibition I received an invitation from Solomon and Whitehead (Guild Prints) to stage an exhibition at their gallery near St Paul's in London in the spring of 1975. I was thrilled and accepted.

The exhibition at Harrods was a great success and I was asked to go back the following year. What a morale booster this was – of course I accepted. I suddenly came face to face with the practical side of events and realised that, having held the exhibition at Harrods in November 1974 and agreed to the Solomon and Whitehead's in May 1975 and the second Harrods exhibition six months later, I was staging three exhibitions in twelve months.

I was still very much involved with the commercial art business at the time and was also demonstrating and lecturing to groups and art societies around the country. During that eighteen-month period, more than at any other time, I needed the self-discipline that I had acquired at school and in the Army, and patience and understanding from my family. Fortunately, I got all that and more. The exhibitions were all very successful and the family managed to keep its sanity.

The following year I held a successful exhibition at Rackhams department store in Birmingham and I was back at Harrods again in 1977 and 1979 (a two-year gap – I had learned my lesson). A practical reason for this two-year gap was that I had been commissioned by Collins to write two books on the subject of learning to paint. In 1981 I was back at Harrods again for another exhibition, and in 1982 I held a one-man exhibition at Hamm-Rhynern in West Germany. Because of all my other commitments I decided not to exhibit in 1983 but I had arranged my next exhibition, again at Harrods, for 1984.

People come back year after year to see and buy my paintings, and we always get a lot of pleasure from discussing my current

work. In fact, each exhibition is like a big reunion party. There is one enthusiastic admirer in particular, who came to one of my early demonstrations and turns up at every exhibition I hold, even though he can't afford the price of my paintings. Another admirer of my work, who lives in the north of England and had been abroad when one of my exhibitions in London opened, flew down immediately on his return. He came to the exhibition, bought two large paintings, then flew straight back home.

There was a rewarding, though slightly embarrassing, moment on the first day of another of my Harrods exhibitions. At one point it seemed that everyone wanted to buy paintings at the same time and there were so many people crowding the gallery that the way was blocked for customers to pass through to the other departments. What a way to get a captive audience!

Diplomacy saved the day on the occasion when two people spotted a painting at the same time and both wanted to buy it. After talking to the two ladies they each went away happily with a picture, leaving the one they had originally decided on still hanging on the wall!

In the summer of 1980 I resigned my position as co-director in the commercial art and design company, which gave me more time for painting and all my other activities. The *Learn to Paint* books were proving successful and I found much of my time was taken up writing and painting for the books.

Author's collection

◀ **Fig. 45** *River Otter, Tipton, Devon*, 38 x 53 cm (15 x 21 in), is a quick freestyle watercolour I painted on the way back from a sketching trip. My attention was caught by the white noticeboard against the dark tree and the sunlit field behind the fence. Notice how I left white paper showing through for the noticeboard

By courtesy of the *Chester Observer*

◀ This photograph was taken on the opening night of my exhibition at the Barclay Art Gallery in Chester in 1973 and shows me with, from left to right, my wife June, the wife of the gallery owner and the Duchess of Westminster

With the benefit of hindsight, I would like to suggest some tips that I consider to be of vital importance to the would-be artist.

The most important thing of all is to be prepared to work hard. There is always someone who is willing to work harder than you. If you are offered the opportunity of having a professional to sell your work to galleries then accept and pay the price – within reason.

If you are not so lucky, be prepared for a long search before you find a gallery that will agree to hang your first painting. Be determined and have faith in yourself – you must be on show. I have found that most galleries will agree to see your work. After all, it is in their interest because, if they refuse, you may go to the next town, another gallery may accept your work and you may turn out to be the next John Constable – and they would have missed out.

Always, without exception, frame your pictures well or have them done professionally. Poor framing can ruin your work. Presentation is very important. Bear in mind, too, that most galleries prefer you to work on standard-size canvas (that is, the stock sizes you can buy from art suppliers).

Plan an exhibition at least six to twelve months ahead. If you have an exhibition early in your career be prepared to do a lot of the organizing yourself. You will usually find that a gallery will offer to sell your paintings first – to test the market – before entertaining any suggestion of a one-man show.

Private collection

CHECKLIST FOR EXHIBITIONS
Date and duration of exhibition?
How many paintings are wanted?
Approximate size of paintings – will they all be large, small or mixed sizes?
Who is doing the framing?
Who is designing and paying for the catalogue?
Who pays for the invitations?
What sort of advertising and who pays?
Is there to be a first-night preview?
Who pays for the reception (drinks, etc.)?

▲ Fig. 46 *Point to Point, Ottery St Mary, Devon*, 29 x 46 cm (11½ x 18 in), was painted in watercolour for the Society of Equestrian Artists' annual exhibition at the Mall Galleries, London, in 1983. I worked from sketches made on the spot and photographs I had taken on that wet and misty day. I worked wet-on-wet after soaking all the areas of the paper except for the wooden fence at the base of the jump, which I wanted left white. I then laid in my first washes, taking care not to cover the wooden fence. As always with a watercolour, I added the detail when the base washes were dry

I have a prepared checklist for one-man exhibitions, shown on the previous page. Naturally, not all the points apply to all galleries or all exhibitions. When I go for my first meeting with a gallery owner, this is the checklist I take. You may find it useful.

I have taken part in many mixed exhibitions over the years. These are simply exhibitions of the work of several artists. You may find that a gallery will involve you in one of these before offering you a one-person show.

In a further attempt at getting your work on show you may like to consider submitting pictures to the professional societies' annual exhibitions held in London. Many of the societies are now household names, for instance, the Royal Academy, the Royal Institute of Oil Painters, the Royal Institute of Painters in Watercolour, the Royal Society of British Artists, the Royal Society of Marine Artists, the Pastel Society, the Society of Women Artists, the Society of Equestrian Artists, the Society of Wildlife Artists and so on, and most of them are open to the public to submit pictures for selection. The Royal Academy's Summer Exhibition is held at the Royal Academy of Arts in Piccadilly; most of the other societies hold their exhibitions in the Mall Galleries or in the Westminster Galleries. The British Watercolour Society's exhibition takes place each year in Ilkley, Yorkshire, and the National Acrylic Painters Association hold theirs at the Royal Birmingham Society of Artists' Gallery.

Figs. 47–50 show some fine art prints that I have had published.

Fig. 47 *Wind and Fire*, reproduced from an acrylic painting which measured 51 x 101 cm (20 x 40 in), was published as a signed, limited edition print of 500 copies, each copy bearing the stamp of the Fine Art Trade Guild. I like the movement of the smoke and the horses in the painting. I get the information for my horses from ploughing matches, country fairs and country museums

Fig. 48 *First Breath of Spring*, reproduced from an acrylic painting, 51 x 76 cm (20 x 30 in), was published in the early 1970s. It was worked from a sketch made near Birmingham. I was driving home from Manchester and we stopped in a lay-by while June fed our baby, Clinton. I wandered off, saw this scene and was inspired to sketch it. I then used the sketch to work on an acrylic painting in my studio.

Fig. 49 *Gathering Mist*, reproduced from an acrylic painting, 61 x 91 cm (24 x 36 in), was inspired by the scene of mist rising one late afternoon as I walked back to the car after a fishing trip

Fig. 50 *Sweet and Dry*, reproduced from an acrylic painting, 51 x 76 cm (20 x 30 in), shows Triggs Lock on the River Wey at Send, near where I used to live in Surrey

▲ **Fig. 47**

By kind permission of Miss Carter Publications

▲ Fig. 48

▲ Fig. 50

▲ Fig. 49

Figs. 48–50 by kind permission of Felix Rosenstiel's Widow & Son Limited

▶ **Fig. 51** In the first edition of the book this Second World War Spitfire was reproduced in black and white. I painted it in oils on canvas in 1966. At that time I enjoyed painting quite a few aeroplanes; the problem is that an aeroplane isn't as easy a subject to find as a landscape!

Private collection

▶ **Fig. 52** *Minnie Celebrates Her Centenary*, reproduced from an acrylic painting 51 x 76 cm (20 x 30 in), was published as a fine art print, 41 x 61 cm (16 x 24 in), in 1981. The 060 saddle tank locomotive was christened Minnie over a hundred years ago. She was built by Fox Walker & Co. of Bristol between 1860 and 1880 and delivered new to Skinningrove Iron Works near Saltburn in Yorkshire where she worked until 1962 when she was displaced by diesel. Minnie was then acquired by a private owner, who was offered a length of track on which she could be stored by the Kent and East Sussex Railway. She now rests at the old Northiam Railway Station in Sussex, still looking proud. The coach was built in 1930 to a Maunsell design and, when I painted the picture, was awaiting restoration. I felt it a fitting tribute to Minnie to paint her in her retirement to celebrate her centenary

Information on these societies can be acquired by writing to the Federation of British Artists, 17 Carlton House Terrace, London SW1Y 5BD, or to the individual society direct. They will supply you with the dates of forthcoming exhibitions, together with the handing-in dates for each one. Generally, you may submit up to six pictures and the handing-in takes place over one or two days, with one day allocated for collecting any unaccepted work.

The Society of Amateur Artists (SAA) was founded in 1992 by June and myself. It was created to encourage, inspire and inform anyone who wants to paint. Annual membership is open to all and enquiries should be addressed to The Society of Amateur Artists, PO Box 50, Newark, Nottinghamshire NG23 5GY.

The first time I became involved in any of the professional societies' annual exhibitions was in 1976 when it was suggested that I submit work to the Royal Society of British Artists. It was not until the 1981 exhibition that I had a painting accepted. The elation I felt was indescribable after so much disappointment each time for five years when my paintings were turned down. It was one of the most important and memorable occasions of my painting career, equal only to the day in 1978 when I was elected a Fellow of the Royal Society of Arts.

ALWYN CRAWSHAW

By kind permission of Felix Rosenstiel's Widow & Son Limited

The Silver Jubilee Fleet Review

In the Queen's Silver Jubilee year, 1977, I was determined to paint one of the many great events that would take place.

I decided on the Silver Jubilee Fleet Review, which was due to be held at Spithead, off Portsmouth, on June 28, when the Queen would review the fleet from on board the Royal Yacht *Britannia*.

The planning and timing of the painting were of paramount importance. The Fleet Review was going to happen only once. I bought a souvenir brochure, newspapers and magazines covering the week's events, to familiarize myself with the scene, and arranged to stay with relatives who live in Gosport.

June and I arrived on the evening before the Review and on the following morning I set off at six o'clock for the seafront. The atmosphere as I walked through Gosport was electrifying. There was activity everywhere and I could feel the excitement and expectancy of the occasion all around me.

I passed quays where small boats and yachts, trimmed with bunting, were being prepared for sea; It really did seem that

◄ **Fig. 53** To sketch a scene covering such a vast area, the first thing I had to consider was where to start and finish on my paper. After studying the scene for a while I began to plan the drawing. Using a 2B pencil on cartridge drawing paper, I positioned the nearest ship (the one just astern of the Royal Yacht in Fig. 54), then proceeded to position the other ships. I was surprised to find fairly soon that I had misread the scale of the scene; if I had continued I would have got only a third of the desired scene on the paper. So back to the drawing board! I decided to use two pages of my sketchbook to give me the desired width and found a scale that would fit the area, with the help of measuring with my pencil. I then drew in the eye level (the horizon) and started the drawing. The aim of the sketch was information: I needed to note the position of the large ships, the type and name of each one (the numbers on their sides were checked through the binoculars), the position of the hundreds of small craft, the direction of the sun and wind and so on. I had not decided on the position I wanted the Royal Yacht to appear in the picture; this would be determined when she sailed past

Private collection

everyone in Gosport that day was involved in the event in some way or other.

I eventually arrived at the seafront. There in front of me was the *Ark Royal* with all the fleet disappearing out of my view behind her. I knew I wouldn't be using this particular scene for my large painting, but I enjoyed sketching there for a while and it prepared me for the rest of the day's work.

My cousin had organized a first-floor room for me at an hotel on the seafront at Lee-on-Solent, from which I could sketch the Review. June and I arrived after breakfast and I set myself up in front of the open window. I started my pencil sketch (I had decided I wasn't going to work in colour), and my excitement grew as I worked, using two pages of my pad (see Fig. 53 on

▲ **Fig. 54** shows the finished acrylic painting, 51 x 152 cm (20 x 60 in). Before I started, the big decision I had to make was regarding the mood of the painting. Was I to cheat and have the sun giving light and shade to the ships and sea, or was I to show that it was a grey and windy day? I overcame the temptation to use artistic licence, which made the work more difficult because,

without light and shade, almost everything is grey. I started by painting the sky. The main colours used in the painting were Coeruleum, Crimson, Cadmium Yellow and White. For the hull of the Royal Yacht, I used Ultramarine Blue, Crimson, a little Cadmium Yellow and White. After the sky I painted the hills in the distance, then the sea, without any detail, and finally I blocked in the

large ships. These became a labour of love at times, working from references for the technical detail. Most of the work on the ships was done with sizes 4 and 2 flat nylon brushes and small sable brushes. I used the same range of brushes for the small craft, which I painted once the large ships were completed large ships were completed

page 56). I took photographs of the ships for reference although, sadly, I didn't have a telephoto lens, but I used binoculars to get close-up information as I sketched.

I finished just before the Royal Yacht *Britannia* came past with the Queen on board. I took some more photographs and marked two pencil lines on my sketch to show the position of the yacht. I could not sketch the yacht herself as she passed by too quickly. Soon after, the weather – which had been overcast all day – turned even worse, and the Isle of Wight disappeared in

heavy mist. But what a day it had been! Sadly, the photographs I had taken turned out to be disappointing because of the lens I had used and also because of the poor light which made the pictures flat. However, I had enough reference from my sketch, my sketching notes and *Jane's Fighting Ships* for technical detail.

The finished painting was done in acrylic colour on canvas 51 x 152 cm (20 x 60 in) (see Figs. 54 and 55) and was hung in my exhibition at Harrods' art gallery in November 1977.

▶ **Fig. 55** shows a detail of the finished painting. I added the darker areas in the sea to liven up the greyness of the water. I left the bunting on the ships until the end otherwise it would have been constantly painted over as I worked on and altered the ships. Notice how the area around the bow of the large warship has been kept uncluttered to give a strong shape to the bows. I kept the bow wave smaller on this ship but emphasized it on the Royal Yacht to help give it even more importance

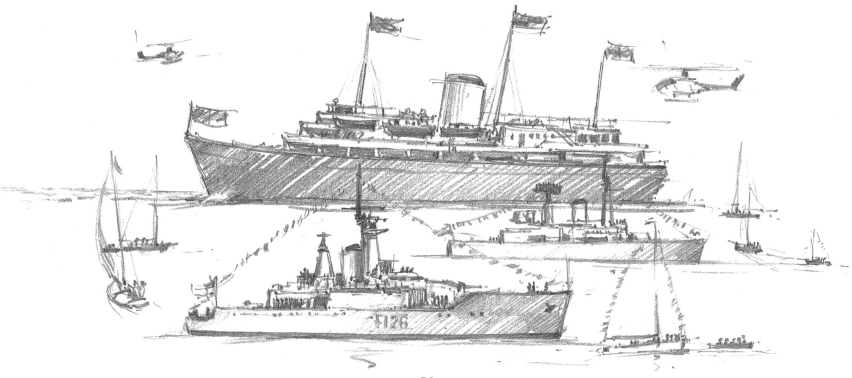

Chapter 4

TEACHING SKILLS & TECHNIQUES

When I am not actually painting a picture, my other natural instinct is to give someone the benefit of my experience through teaching. I find it very satisfying to help other people to enjoy themselves through painting.

In 1970, by absolute chance, one of the visitors to the stationer's and art supplier's where I was holding my first exhibition was Tom Rowney, who was then chairman of George Rowney and Company, as the paint manufacturers were then known. He saw my work, for which I had used their Cryla colours, the Rowney acrylic artists' colours, and liked it. Lady luck had struck again! He invited me to the Rowney headquarters at Bracknell in Berkshire where I was met by the late Royston Davies, who helped me so much during that time and continued to advise me for many years to come.

After that first meeting it was suggested that I might like to represent Rowney as one of their official demonstrators and lecturers. I was very flattered and accepted. I remember being a little apprehensive at the time as I had never seen a painting demonstration, let

alone undertaken one. I gave a great deal of thought to that first demonstration and eventually worked out a presentation to show painting techniques using acrylic colours. Armed with all my equipment I set off for my first demonstration at Hove in Sussex. The time, thought and preplanning paid off and it was a success. To this day I have kept to the same format, apart from

▶ **Fig. 56** is a watercolour, 38 x 53 cm (15 x 21 in), that I painted for a demonstration in the summer of 1983, when taking a masterclass at the annual Sidmouth Visual Arts Festival in Devon. I decided to demonstrate a watercolour of the sea front but didn't quite realize what I was letting myself in for until I was sitting on the beach with all the students and passers-by watching me and waiting for me to start. I looked at my blank piece of Whatman paper with the sun glaring on it, then at the complicated and busy scene in front of me and felt very lonely. But, within minutes, I was off and I talked and

painted for about three hours. The important part of the painting was the drawing, which took about an hour. Before starting to paint, I decided I would leave white paper to show through for most of the boats on the beach and the white buildings. I then painted the sky and distance, working down in washes of colour. I explained to the students that you can put another wash or brush stroke over a previously painted area and make it darker if you wish, but you can't make it lighter. So if you are not confident, work your tones light and darken where necessary as the picture builds up

Author's collection

introducing new materials and updating techniques. The one thing I didn't bargain for was shaky hands, through nerves. Having taken the tops off the tubes of paint and squeezed the paint onto my palette, I found that my hands were shaking so much I couldn't replace the tops. Fortunately, I did all this before the demonstration started so I don't think anyone noticed. After I had got over the first few nerve-racking minutes I settled down and even enjoyed it.

My basic objective, when demonstrating, is to get the audience involved. As I paint I talk about the techniques I am using and I get the audience to ask questions and make comments. So throughout the demonstration there is a constant conversation. I keep it light by relating stories of my painting and demonstrating experiences but I also try to get across as much practical information as

possible. Usually a demonstration lasts two to three hours, depending on the premises they are held in or sometimes on the goodwill of the caretaker.

Since that first demonstration, I have travelled extensively throughout the country and abroad, imparting my knowledge to members of art societies, and at in-store and trade fair demonstrations. I have held demonstrations in public libraries, church halls, village halls, schoolrooms and colleges, in freezing cold and unbearable heat, in perfect lighting and in lighting so poor I almost had to guess the colours I was mixing.

For instance, in the early 1970s when I was demonstrating for a week in the store Beales of Bournemouth, I had to cope with constant power cuts. By law I was allowed only one 100-watt bulb hanging from a high ceiling. This was obviously useless for my purposes (mind you, everyone else was in the same boat), so I worked for my audience with a torch in one hand and my brush in the other – the show had to go on! Another difficult demonstration was one I did at Guildford in Surrey in the 1970s. This took place in an old, well-preserved building that had highly polished floorboards. I sat down at my easel but when I put my first brush stroke on the canvas the easel slid away from me. I spent the whole evening with my legs wrapped around the easel to prevent it from slipping as I painted – not the most comfortable of positions in which to work!

▶ **Fig. 57** *A Devon River*, 51 x 76 cm (20 x 30 in), was painted in acrylics on canvas from a watercolour painted for a demonstration near my home. I wanted to capture the atmosphere of a hot day and show a clear, rippling Devon river. I painted about six washes of colour on the river to achieve the clarity of the water right down to the stones on the bed, using a mix of Ultramarine Blue, Crimson, Burnt Umber and Bright Green. With acrylics you don't need to wait too long for a wash to dry before applying the next one

By kind permission of Omell Galleries, London and Windsor

I have demonstrated to hundreds of different art societies throughout the country and I have been asked back so often that many of them have become like second homes. I am invited to open their annual exhibitions or to judge their painting competitions, and June and I are regularly invited to their Christmas parties.

I meet so many old friends every time and usually come away having made a lot of new ones. Sometimes I meet up with people I last saw at a demonstration years before and hundreds of miles away. I'm often surprised and very flattered at the distances people travel to attend my demonstrations. When I was demonstrating at an arts festival in Battle (my old home town) I had an audience of over 150, some of whom had travelled from London and the east coast to see me. I am always amazed at how many people at a demonstration have read my books. When I arrive they seem to know more about me than I do! During all my years of demonstrating – and some demonstrations are booked two years in advance – I have only ever missed two. And I can honestly say that I have loved them all!

A very rewarding project I have also been involved in is running private art courses. The initial idea was to run the courses in an outbuilding we had converted for the purpose when we moved to Metcombe, near Ottery St Mary in Devon in 1981. Soon after it was completed, we met the owner of the Salston Hotel, which was nearby, and discovered that

he and his wife owned many of my paintings. He asked if I would be interested in running art courses at his hotel and I thought it was a marvellous idea. For many years I ran weekend and week-long courses for up to fifteen students there. These were very exciting, and also rewarding as you could see changes in people's attitudes and work in just a few days. My converted outbuilding was sadly neglected – I only had time to run a few courses in it.

June was very much involved with me on these courses. She was the perfect public relations officer, student and eventually teacher. She painted along with the other students and helped to put them at ease very quickly. We worked both in the studio and – weather permitting – outside and I was with the students constantly during the day and evening, helping with their particular problems, demonstrating techniques and generally being the target for hundreds of questions. Sometimes we worked late into the evening and at the end of a long day we were all happily exhausted. But the following day we were ready for more.

I would like to offer a few tips for students attending courses. If you are a beginner I would suggest you use watercolours. The equipment is easy to carry around with you and you may feel happier working reasonably inconspicuously with just a pad on your knee. If you are going out on a painting trip take as little equipment as you can. I have known some students on my

▶ **Figs. 58–61** These four watercolours, each 13 x 19 cm (5 x 7½ in), are a constant reminder of a New Year resolution I made – and broke – in 1983. I resolved to paint a small, half-hour watercolour every day. I thought it was a marvellous idea: it would keep me in trim, I would have plenty of work to show students and I estimated that I would paint about 250 in a year. The net result in that year is the four paintings shown here. My excuse was that I had been too busy working on other paintings and fulfilling all my commitments. Fig. 58 was painted during a walk ten minutes from home; notice the white farmhouse – I left it unpainted. It was bitterly cold that day but it was worth the time I spent painting it because I achieved the desired result and recorded the scene as a simple statement. Figs. 59 and 60 showed the view from my studio window, and Fig. 61 was painted as I sat in the car waiting for June to come back from shopping. I cherish these four simple watercolours and I won't part with them. I would recommend the exercise to anyone who loves painting, whether you are a beginner or a competent artist. However, I suggest you paint more than four!

Figs. 58–61: Author's collection

▲ Fig. 58

▲ Fig. 60

▼ Fig. 59

▼ Fig. 61

courses to turn up with so much equipment that by the time they have got it all to their painting spot and set it up, they are exhausted and it is almost time to go home! Do try to be as mobile as possible. And one last important hint: make sure you have enough clothing on. When you are outside you can always take something off if it gets warmer but you will be very miserable and your work will suffer if you are cold.

Another way I have been able to pass on information on skills and techniques is by writing books. In 1978, I was asked by Collins to write two books on painting for their *Learn to Paint* series. They were to be instructional books, one on painting in acrylics and the other in watercolours. Not only was I to write the books I was also to devise a format for a series that would include books on the different painting mediums and different aspects of painting, written by a variety of artists.

Eventually the format was designed, Collins liked it and I started a very busy six months writing and painting for the books. They were a great success. I have now completed eight and the series is selling all over the world. It gives me enormous pleasure to think that so many people are learning from my experiences.

I receive letters regularly from people who have read my books and have been inspired to start or to progress further with their painting. One reader from Belgium wrote with great enthusiasm about my watercolour

By courtesy of Brooke Photographic

▲ At the first International Bicton Carriage Driving Trials, which were held near my home, I was invited to judge the Concours d'Elégance and I donated an equestrian painting for the first prize. The photograph shows me presenting it to the winner

book and asking to come on one of my painting courses. Another reader, from South Africa, wrote full of praise for the help that my books had given him and his friends. A very charming lady from Canada, whom I met while she was on a visit to England, told

me of the immense pleasure and helpful instruction that she and her painting friends gained from reading my books. I also received a letter from a reader in Kalgoorlie in Australia, who was very flattering about the books and wanted to thank me for what she had learnt from them. She lives in the outback and told me the nearest shop where she can buy the books is 400 miles away. When I experience these encounters with my readers, I get a tremendous feeling of elation.

Over the years I have also written articles for the magazines, *The Artist* and *Leisure Painter*. Once again, it is a way that I can offer my experiences as a guide to others. But I do stress that word 'guide'. All artists paint differently and are looking for different results. However, if I can give inspiration to encourage people to enter the fascinating world of painting or help people over a painting block then I have succeeded – and if I offer more to some students then that is a bonus.

I have found that fear is the biggest hurdle some people have to overcome in order to start painting. They feel there is a great mystery surrounding painting and they are afraid of it. But it is a fact that we are all afraid of the unknown. For instance, I know nothing about a television set and the thought of learning how to build one terrifies me. But if the 'mysteries' were explained and I was taught all the stages in a logical order, I would be able to make a passable attempt at putting all the pieces together. The same applies to painting.

By kind permission of *Leisure Painter*

Private collection

▲ **Fig. 62** *From Heaton Park, Manchester,* 38 x 51 cm (15 x 20 in), is one of the watercolours I painted for a series of articles I wrote for *Leisure Painter* magazine in 1983. I did very little drawing, simply sketching in the cooling towers, the main chimneys and some lines for the fields and rows of houses. I then started painting. The housing estate is only suggested, to allow the eye to travel over it and settle on the cooling towers in the middle distance. The only red used is Crimson Alizarin. For the houses I added Cadmium Yellow for the warmer areas and French Ultramarine for the shadow areas

▲ **Fig. 63** *Sidmouth, Devon,* 38 x 51 cm (15 x 20 in). This watercolour, painted on Bockingford paper, was another painting I did as a demonstration. The problem I needed to overcome on this occasion was that the yachts were being made ready for sea. At one time I couldn't see the distant buildings because of yacht sails. When I had finished the drawing, there were no yachts there at all, they were all at sea. I made the decision at the drawing stage to show only two. Naturally, it is impossible to keep changing a drawing as yachts come and go. Once the decision is made, you must stick to it. At one point, there were at least eight sails up and blowing in the wind and they looked great, but I could not start the drawing again

In the spring of 1981, I found myself involved in something with enough mysteries to make my hair stand on end! I received a phone call from a television producer working on the BBC *Pebble Mill at One* programme, asking if I would be interested in appearing on the programme in two days' time to talk about my painting techniques. The programme was to go out national and live. I was to stay overnight in Birmingham, near the studios, and the programme was to be broadcast the following day. June was invited as well. I don't know whether they had sensed that I needed moral support – if they had, they were right!

I prepared some work to take up with me, then we set off from home and arrived at the hotel in the early evening. In the morning we went to the studio and I prepared my painting equipment, which included a Stay-Wet palette with the colours squeezed out on it. (This type of palette keeps acrylic colours wet almost indefinitely, as long as you keep the lid on it when you are not working.) My easel was set up with a partially-completed painting on it, which I was to work on for about three minutes in front of the camera at the end of the interview. A camera was directed at the palette so that viewers would be able to see the brush in close-up mixing colours as I painted.

Once this was done I had a chat with Bob Langley, the presenter who was to interview me. He quickly put me at ease, which impressed me enormously as I had thought it would have taken knock-out drops to calm me down! He gave me the cues for the start and finish of the interview, at which point, he explained, the screen would show some of my paintings. There was then just over an hour to go before the programme started. I stood, sat, walked around, talked to June, unaware of all the activity that was going on around me.

I was terrified. Eventually the studio lights went on and the programme started. I had another twenty minutes to wait. The time came and I was led very quietly through the audience and onto the set. I sat down in position and a microphone was threaded up my jumper and fastened to my shirt front.

ARUNDEL, CASTLE, SUSSEX 1 NOV 83

▶ **Fig. 64** *Noss Mayo*, 25 x 30 cm (10 x 12 in), oil on primed hardboard. I hadn't painted in oils for about four months when I did this painting on location. I was very excited and settled down and started painting. Within ten minutes several people, who recognized me through my books, gathered round, so the painting finished up as a demonstration!

ALWYN CRAWSHAW

There was no way out now! With seconds to go and in an effort to calm myself, I picked up a brush to mix some paint on the palette. Lady luck had deserted me! I had forgotten to put the lid on my palette and the studio lights had dried out all my paints. There was no way I would be able to do the painting scheduled for the last three minutes of the interview.

Suddenly I was aware of Bob Langley sitting in front of me and giving me my cue to start the interview, with the cameras on both of us. My mind was split in two: one half was answering Bob's questions and the other was trying to work out how I was going to cope with the inevitable disaster. I decided the only way was to tell the truth and make light of the situation when the time came. Once I had made my decision I was able to relax. My nerves disappeared as I found myself doing something I was very accustomed to – talking about painting. I was well into the swing of things when suddenly Bob uttered the sentence that was the cue for the end of the interview and the screen showed my paintings. It was all over!

Directly the show had finished the producer apologised profusely for the fact that I had not been allowed the three minutes for painting the picture. The reason was that the previous interview had over-run, so my time had had to be cut. I said it was perfectly all right and that I fully understood. Lady luck had returned – but hadn't she left it late!

Since that time, I have become more used to appearing on television. I am glad to say

▶ Time for a criticism of students' still life work undertaken on one of the painting courses I ran at the Salston Hotel, near my home in Devon

By courtesy of Jeff Bowden

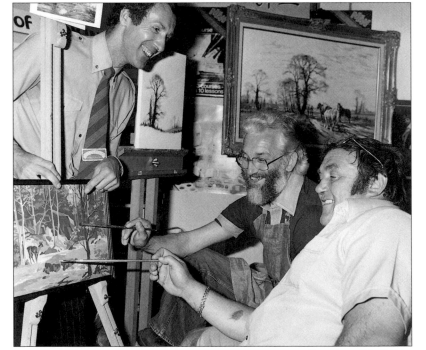

By courtesy of Tim Aldridge

◀ At a two-day demonstration I gave in the 1970s at an Ideal Home Exhibition in Woking, Surrey, the comedian Les Dawson was autographing his newly-published book on the stand next to mine. It wasn't too long before he was practising his hand at painting, with me trying to help!

that, over the years, as the mystery of it has disappeared, most of the fear has gone, too.

Similarly, once you try painting you will soon see that there is no mystery to it. But do try. At your first attempt you will conquer some of your nerves so that your next attempt will be much easier – and it will get progressively easier with time. And it doesn't matter how old you are when you start – painting has no age limit. The late Helen Bradley MBE started painting when she was sixty-five!

▲ This photograph shows me demonstrating a watercolour painting for a group from the Honiton Art Society in Devon. The sunshades tell the story: it was a gloriously hot day, but that can make watercolour painting difficult as the paint dries so quickly. One answer is to use plenty of water with your paint

An Outing to Halsway Manor

In the hot summer of 1983 my sister Shirley, who was then head of the art department at Manchester College of Education, contacted me to say she was planning to take a class of students to Halsway Manor in Somerset. As it is only about an hour and a half's journey from my home, she wondered whether I would be prepared to meet her there for a day to give an outdoor demonstration. On a beautiful summer's morning June and I set off on the journey. As we got nearer to the manor, the mist that had begun to appear earlier became thicker and the hills in the distance were disappearing.

When we arrived at the manor, Shirley and the students were beginning to despair as they watched the views being swallowed up by the mist. I was disappointed too, for on the journey all my thoughts had been directed to painting a landscape. I then made a brave decision: I would paint the manor. There was a buzz of excitement – none of the students had seen a subject like that being tackled before. What they didn't realize was that I had never tackled a subject like that for a demonstration. It was a huge challenge.

◀ I wonder what Gene Kelly would have made of this situation! After those first warning drops, I ended up somewhere under the umbrella painting in the rain. It wasn't as heavy as in the film, but it was still enough to make watercolour painting difficult

The first job was to find a painting spot. I wandered around for almost an hour in search of it, familiarizing myself with the building and the surroundings. I had several problems to solve. Not only had I to find a good view to paint, in a spot with enough room for the students to watch my demonstration, I also had to make sure that the view I chose had enough light, without the help of the sun, to give contrast to the building. (The sun never did come out!) More than any other subject, a building needs light and dark to show form, especially when you are painting it for a demonstration. Eventually I found the spot and all the students gathered round claiming their places, some sitting, some standing.

After discussing the preliminaries I started the drawing for what was to be a watercolour painting. This is the most important part of a painting of this nature. If the drawing isn't good the painting will never succeed, especially if you are working with watercolours.

▲ **Fig. 65** is my drawing of the manor, 38 x 51 cm (15 x 20 in), on Whatman paper. Having established the eye level, I worked from the right of the building, drawing vertical lines to indicate the main sections. Once this was done, I drew in the roofs, the tops of the building walls and the garden wall. I then worked on the detail – the doors, windows, garden steps and so on – until I had enough drawing for my painting. Once a drawing is completed I normally like to take time to reflect on it while looking at the subject. Because of limited time during a demonstration this isn't usually possible, but I recommend students to do it. I didn't draw in the trees as I wasn't sure that I wanted them in the finished painting. In the event, I included them to give strength to the building

▲ This detail of the finished painting shows how I made the right-hand doorway the darkest spot on the manor house, to help stabilize the building and give it a point of interest

▶ This photograph shows me well under way with the painting. At this stage, I was feeling quite relaxed, as the drawing was done and most of the important washes had been applied. In fact, I was indulging myself by adding some detail!

▶ **Fig. 66** shows the finished painting, 38 x 51 cm (15 x 20 in). I started by painting the sky, using a wash of Coeruleum Blue, Crimson Alizarin and Yellow Ochre and a No. 10 round sable brush, which I used for the whole picture, except for such small detail as the windows, doors, suggested stonework, etc., for which I used a No. 6 sable brush. I then worked on the main walls of the manor, leaving the windows unpainted, using Yellow Ochre, Crimson Alizarin and a touch of French Ultramarine for the shadow areas. Then I painted in the roofs, using stronger tones of the sky colours. When the walls were dry I put another wash of colour on the shadow areas to give dimension and form to the building. I then put in some of the foliage using Hooker's Green No. 1, Yellow

Ochre, Crimson Alizarin and French Ultramarine. The next step was to paint the windows. This can be difficult because if they are painted too dark they stand out dramatically and if they are too pale they disappear. I worked first with a pale wash of Coeruleum Blue and Crimson Alizarin, leaving small areas of white paper to show through. While the wash was wet I ran in darker colour on some windows, made by adding a little Payne's Grey to the mix. I painted more dark colour on some of the windows when the wash was dry. Once the windows were completed the painting was in a stable position; it had shape and form. I continued adding detail where I thought the picture needed it, but tried to keep an overall balance. Too much work in one spot could damage the visual flow of the painting

After about an hour and a half the drawing was finished and we took a break for a picnic lunch on the lawn. The mist was getting even worse as I started the painting and soon it turned into fine drizzle. What a catastrophe for a watercolour! Within minutes the students had found an umbrella and a plastic mac, which they held over my head and the painting. Amid much humour and comments about our terrible English weather we carried on enjoying the class (see the photograph on page 72) and I managed to complete the painting.

When I look at a completed demonstration painting I often find there are areas that I would have changed or done very differently had I been working on my own. In a demonstration the amount of time I have to reflect on my work is limited and my concentration is often focused more on teaching techniques and showing my approach to working than on the actual painting. However, I usually turn any weaknesses or errors in a painting to teaching advantage by pointing them out and discussing them with the students.

Fig. 66 shows the picture, which has not been touched since that day. Incidentally, as we drove home that evening the sun came out and the mist cleared!

HALSWAY MANOR — SOMERSET
DEMONSTRATION

Author's collection

Chapter 5

THE CHALLENGE OF PAINTING

Our move to Devon in 1981 was an attempt to get away from it all and to find more time for my one obsession – painting. Not only was I in search of a quieter life in which to undertake my work, I also wanted the luxury of being able to open my doors onto glorious painting views.

Just a little over a decade previously, when our son, Clinton, was born, we had bought a house by the beach at Bracklesham Bay in Sussex with the idea of using it as a place to escape to for a couple of days at a time as a family and where I could paint uninterrupted. I turned one of the bedrooms into a studio and painted many pictures of that part of Sussex during that time.

As a family we had some memorable times there, but with the upkeep and the travelling involved, I hadn't really solved the problem of giving myself more time for painting. So, in 1979, we made the decision to move into the country, lock, stock and barrel, and eventually set up home in Devon.

Of course, things never work out quite the way we think they will and the biggest drawback to my Utopia is always me! I

▶ **Fig. 67** *The Blue Fishing Boat*, 61 x 91 cm (24 x 36 in), was painted in oils on canvas. I worked quite freely from a detailed pencil sketch. I used a similar pencil sketch for Fig. 68 on page 78. The paintings and drawings reproduced in this chapter are amongst my favourites, many evoking fond memories

realize now that wherever I lived I would be busy. If I were to get away from it all in the Outer Hebrides I would find enough to keep myself occupied – even if it were just counting the sheep for the sake of it.

However, at least all my energies were now put into painting and its allied subjects. Since moving to Devon I have written three more books in the *Learn to Paint* series, been involved in television and radio programmes and had exhibitions in London and Germany.

In describing some of the events of my life, let me stress that I am relating a very personal story. Some successful artists lead a much quieter life, others an even fuller life, than I do; some plod along while others race

Private collection

Author's collection

through. I know some artists who dislike talking to the public and some who fight shy of appearing at their own exhibitions, and they are all successful in their own right. We all achieve our goals in very different ways. I simply hope that my thoughts and conclusions may help you to gain an insight into one artist's approach to his work.

I have always had to paint to earn money to live, which has meant painting for a market. During the years when I worked in a commercial art studio, all my thoughts and energies went into designing mainly for the housewife: most of my work ended up on the supermarket shelves or in newspaper advertisements. There was little time to indulge in the luxury of painting what I wanted, knowing that I didn't have to earn money from my pictures. If you have to earn a living from your paintings you have to paint for a market that will buy them. However, if you are to progress you must also find time for experimental painting. An artist's formative years should be spent painting with all mediums and observing and experimenting.

There are many different markets that artists work for, ranging from sophisticated galleries showing abstract and avant-garde works of art, to the holiday trade, where the artists sell from their own workshops direct to the public. These two types of artists are poles

▲ **Fig. 68** *Exmouth at Low Tide*, 18 x 42 cm (7 x 16½ in), was painted in acrylics on primed hardboard. I love this part of Exmouth – it is a complicated jumble of colours and shapes – and in the painting I particularly like the late afternoon sun on the church spire. I made a point of finding one boat – the large blue one – that I could work on with a little more strength and detail, to hold the eye in the confusion of all the other craft. Notice how the reds in the painting are toned down, to keep them in the middle distance. This painting was exhibited at the Royal Society of British Artists' annual exhibition in London in 1982

Private collection

apart in their approach to painting and selling, but they are both playing an important rôle in the art world and, above all, they have found a market for their individual talents.

I thrive on painting pictures but I enjoy just as much the knowledge that I am painting for the pleasure of others. When I am at my exhibitions I feel so elated by the enjoyment people are obviously deriving from my work. I shall never forget seeing a lady standing in front of one of my paintings with tears of sheer joy running down her face. To paint something that can release that kind of emotion is indescribably rewarding.

I am invariably asked at exhibitions: 'How long did it take you to do that painting?' My

▲ **Fig. 69** *Study of a Gate*, 15 x 20 cm (6 x 8 in), was drawn during a walk near my home. Before all the wooden gates disappear, I would like to travel around and draw a selection. A series of drawings showing the way gates are hung, fastened, twisted, broken, made and positioned would make an interesting study of the countryside

▲ **Fig. 70** *Snow at Metcombe, Devon*, 20 x 25 cm (8 x 10 in), was painted in acrylics on a primed plywood panel. I made a pencil sketch outside and painted it in my studio. The weak sunlight on the snow in the foreground was achieved by first painting all the foreground snow in a low, cool key, using a predominance of White, Ultramarine Blue,

Crimson and Raw Umber, and then adding a warm white colour made up of White, Crimson and Cadmium Yellow. The shadows of the branches were then painted over this light area with a small sable brush, using Ultramarine Blue, Crimson and just a little Cadmium Yellow. I kept the red roof in a low key by mixing a little Ultramarine Blue with Crimson

79

usual answer is: 'Sixty years' (or whatever age I am at the time) 'and two days. Sixty years' experience and two days to paint the picture.'

I like to reach as many people as I can with my work, so I am very much in favour of fine art prints, as long as they are of good quality. Of course, they are only reproductions, but just imagine how many people would not have seen Constable's or Turner's work if it had not been reproduced.

I remember so vividly buying my first print on one of my last monthly trips to the Constable room at the National Gallery before going into the Army. It was *The Haywain* and over the ensuing years it gave me more pleasure than I can describe.

The people owning original paintings are the lucky ones but they are few in number; prints of an artist's work reach thousands. I am sure that the reason for the greater public participation and interest in art over the last thirty-five years is the increase in the reproduction of pictures in art books and as fine art prints, calendars and greetings cards.

Finding a print publisher that will accept your paintings for reproduction could involve you in a greater search than finding a gallery that will hang your work. (You will find the names of print publishers, together with other useful information, in *The Writers' and Artists' Year Book*, which is published annually.) I can only suggest that you persevere. I tried eight print publishers over a period of about a year before I had my first

▶ **Fig. 71** *Bert and Daisy,* 19 x 24 cm (7½ x 9½ in), is a watercolour painted from a pencil sketch done at a ploughing match. I made a careful drawing of the horses, then let the paint 'do its own thing' within the confines of my drawing. When doing a freestyle study of something with a lot of shape, form and detail, I have to discipline myself first to loosen up and only broadly suggest the detail

Author's collection

◀ **Fig. 72** is a detail from an acrylic painting, 51 x 101 cm (20 x 40 in), worked from a series of pencil sketches I made at a country fair in Whimple, Devon. I also took some colour photographs for reference of technical detail because I find that, no matter how many sketches you make on the spot of a mechanical object such as a steamroller, when you come to do the painting, there is invariably some necessary detail that has been missed. Notice how the white of the marquee in the background is used to silhouette the front of the steamroller and the figures. This adds a little drama to the scene

Private collection

▶ **Fig. 73** is an acrylic painting, 51 x 101 cm (20 x 40 in), that has many memories for me. It was one of my first large acrylic paintings and was worked from drawings made off the Strand in London just behind where I used to work in my first job as a commercial artist. It is also one of the paintings that I take as an example of acrylic work on most of my demonstrations. Looking at the picture now, I feel the trunk of the plane tree is too prominent; it would help if there were some leaves to break up the straight lines. I would also like to see a little more variation in the brick colours, but I like the sunlit ground, the steps and the white building in the distance against the sky. I think I would be happier with one or two people, or even some London pigeons, to add a little life to the picture

Author's collection

Private collection

◀ **Fig. 74** *Sunshades*, 41 x 51cm (16 x 20 in), is an acrylic painting worked from a sketch made as I sunbathed on the beach during a holiday at Bournemouth. At the time I had no intention of using the sketch for a painting – I simply enjoyed sketching. A couple of years later I found the sketch when I was looking through my sketchbooks and had the urge to paint it. I wasn't concerned about toning down the reds in this painting, as I had been for those in Figs. 68 and 70 on pages 78 and 79; they are in the foreground and, together with the yellow of the sunshades, they are the focal point of the picture. I have purposely not painted in the horizon, to give the impression of a heat haze

RUSSELL, 6 WEEKS.

painting accepted for reproduction. Then it was eighteen months before the print came onto the market. It was a slow business, but the reward was a great sense of achievement.

What is a successful artist? There must be many definitions based on people's different needs and ambitions. For me a successful artist is one who earns enough money for his needs by painting what he enjoys and who receives recognition for his endeavours from fellow artists.

I don't believe you have to be born with the talent for painting. If you have a natural talent this helps enormously but it is not

The figures (above and opposite) are pencil sketches from some of my sketchbooks. It is very frustrating when you see something that inspires you but don't have your sketchbook with you. Where possible, always try to keep one handy to capture those moments. For the sketch (above left),

I was caught out but June (who always carries a sketchbook in her handbag) came to the rescue and lent me hers. I did this while we were sitting outside a café just off Russell Square in London and managed to finish it a few minutes before it started to rain! The sketch (above) has had

to be included as it is of our first grandchild Russell, at six weeks old. I drew the sketch with a 3B pencil on cartridge drawing paper. It took about ten minutes and then the baby woke up – trouble! On the opposite page (top left) are three quick sketches of Nigel as he photographed me for

one of my books. I saw and sketched the Morris Minor in a car park in England; the boat was sketched while June and I were in Majorca, visiting a friend. Finally, I simply couldn't resist the opportunity of capturing Big Ben while it was receiving a face-lift when I visited London in 1983

82

▲ **Fig. 75**

▼ **Fig. 76**　▲ **Fig. 77**

Figs. 75–77: Private collection, Australia

Figs. 75–77 The three paintings on this page are all watercolours, each measuring 38 x 51cm (15 x 20 in), of cricket matches that I painted one Bank Holiday weekend. I approached all the scenes in the same way. I drew the picture first without the cricketers, then I watched the match until I had a good idea of the position in which I wanted the players, to make a good composition, and I drew them in. I then painted the picture, leaving out the cricketers until it was almost complete. Then I brought the cricketers to life by painting a dark blob on each head for hair or a cap and, with a small sable brush, carefully adding a little tonal work to give them their form. Careful planning is essential. and I always take time to study the scene first. It doesn't matter how long this takes; I believe it is the most important part of a painting. These three watercolours were painted for an English landscape exhibition held in 1980 by John Birch in Croydon, Surrey. They were all bought by one person and the last I heard of them they were hanging in Australia

► **Fig. 78** *Steam at Dartmouth*, 25 x 30 cm (10 x 12 in), oil on primed hardboard. This is one of my favourite small freestyle oil paintings. I did a very quick pencil sketch of this steam train and also took some photographs. It is one of the engines that the Paignton and Dartmouth Steam Railway use from Paignton to Dartmouth and back along the beautiful Devon coast. I painted it very freely and didn't fall into the trap, when using a photograph as a guide, of overpainting and adding too much detail. At first, I felt that the distant hill was too strong against the sky but decided it provided a good diagonal line to balance the strong lines of the platform and the roof. Notice how they all converge roughly in a light area around the top of the engine. I feel this gives strength to the painting

Author's collection

Private collection

essential. Even a natural talent has to be worked on and fostered. To paint means to observe, to know how to mix colours, to be able to see three-dimensional objects and translate them into a two-dimensional drawing or painting; to be able to visualize and to create your visions on paper. These are all skills that must be learnt and they can be if they are taken stage by stage.

Remember that painting is a job of work and the harder you work at it, generally speaking, the more you will progress. Some years ago I was commissioned to do some paintings in Wales. During my stay there I climbed mountains, crossed rivers and generally worked very hard in cold weather at finding the best locations to paint. One day I visited the local village shop and got into conversation with the assistant. She asked me what I was doing in the area and when I told her I was painting pictures she asked: 'Do you do it for a living?' 'Yes,' I replied. 'Oh, you are lucky,' she said. 'I wish I could

◄ **Fig. 79** is a detail from *Off for Milking*, 41 x 61 cm (16 x 24 in). I painted this on an unbearably hot day. I drew a pencil sketch outside and painted in my studio. I used light against dark to make a strong point in the picture: the dust thrown up by the cows' silhouettes them and emphasizes the cow's head on the right. For the patches of sunlight I painted the road first in shadow, then added areas of a warm light colour, made up of Cadmium Yellow, Crimson and White

Private collection

◄ **Fig. 80** *Out of the Woods*, 75 x 50 cm (30 x 20 in), is a watercolour painting on Bockingford paper. When I painted this picture, I felt I wanted to express my feelings that the winter was over and it was now early spring. In fact, I felt good. I painted it in the studio and worked large – this gave me the freedom to let the brush and colours flow. I was happy with the result and remember feeling really elated when I had finished it

ASH TREE FROM STUDIO WINDOW JULY '81

▲ **Fig. 81** *Study of an Ash Tree*, 28 x 23 cm (11 x 9 in), was drawn from my studio window. I used a 2B pencil on cartridge drawing paper

◀ **Fig. 82** *Seven is your lucky number, but...*, 38 x 50 cm (15 x 20 in). I approached this watercolour painting, which I did on Waterford 300 lb Rough paper, in an entirely different way to the one opposite. I wanted to paint the horses carefully, therefore I was more restricted in my brush strokes. But above all I wanted to capture the atmosphere of a wet, misty winter afternoon. The soft colours and indistinct background help to give this illusion

Author's collection

do that instead of working.' Well, take it from me, if you are going to earn a living from painting, you will be working – and very hard – but you will enjoy it too.

My recipe for how to be a successful artist is as follows. Learn to draw and learn to observe life. Teach yourself to see life as a drawing or painting; for instance, when you look at the sky or the corner of a room, work out in your mind how you would paint it. Work from nature – she is the greatest teacher. If, for any reason, you leave nature alone and work from your own imagination always go back; just as a car has to have a service, so your imagintion must be serviced with real life. To begin with, work with all the painting mediums you can. Work small, very large, in black and white, or using only

▶ **Fig. 83** *Salisbury Cathedral*, 25 x 30 cm (10 x 12 in), oil on primed hardboard. I painted this on the spot in very soft light. The trees and water were painted very simply to let the eye go past them into the picture and up to the cathedral. The water was worked with a 'thin' paint over Yellow Ochre underpainting, leaving it showing through in places. The reflections give the illusion of water

▶ **Fig. 84** *Potato Pickers, St. Clement, Jersey*, 40 x 50 cm (16 x 20 in), oil on canvas. I sketched this scene first in watercolour, then worked this oil painting from it. The rows of potatoes were quite a challenge, but variations of greens and earth colours helped to make the field flat but interesting

Fig. 83: Author's collection; Fig. 84: Private collection

a few colours, paint every conceivable subject; above all, keep working in every spare moment and enjoy painting in all its different forms. You will find that your own particular aptitudes will develop naturally. You could be brilliant at drawing in black and white, or your strong point could be figure work or composition or colour. Whatever it is, it will be your own particular talent throughout your artistic career. It doesn't mean you won't be good at anything else but you will find that this natural ability will always be your greatest asset.

During this formative period you will find that some of the avenues you explore are not for you, but by giving yourself a thorough grounding you will emerge with a definite 'feel' for the type of work you want to do. Don't despair if you think it's never going to

▲ **Fig. 85**

▲ **Fig. 87**

▼ **Fig. 86**

Fig. 85 by kind permission of Mrs N Dumbleton; Fig 86: Private collection; Fig. 87: Author's collection

Fig. 85 *A Walk in the Sun*, 38 x 50 cm (15 x 20 in), watercolour on Bockingford 200 lb. June and I have often walked down this lane, and I painted it very freely from memory, in the studio. The shadows on the path and trees help to create sunlight

Fig. 86 *My Studio, Devon*, 35 x 48 cm (14 x 19 in), watercolour on Whatman paper

200 lb Not. I had never thought of painting this view of my studio before, but one afternoon I was tremendously inspired and had to do it there and then. The drawing of the door and window was very important. These had to be correct, as they were the main features of the painting. I also left them as unpainted white paper. I then painted the inside of the studio and

finally I put a light grey wash over the windows. This left the open doorway lighter in tone, making the glass look more realistic

Fig. 87 *Preparations for the Big Day*, 41 x 51 cm (16 x 20 in), is an acrylic painting capturing that magic moment early in the morning when the sun breaks through the mist, promising a great day ahead

Fig. 88 I do enjoy sketching animals but find that sometimes when I draw them they look very wooden and I am fighting to draw every line. On other occasions, they seem to fall off my pencil and run around the sketchbook! But it is worth all the poor days for some of those magical moments

happen to you. When I left art school I was at the experimental stage. During my commercial art period I was conditioned to (and had to learn) a specific type of art. When I started painting pictures again in earnest it took me nearly two years to find my subject – landscape – and the style in which I wanted to paint it.

Be aware of the fact that right up to the very last picture you paint you are still learning – so accept constructive criticism. In fact, invite criticism of your work, from lay people as well as professionals. You must see your work through other people's eyes. Once you have found your way of painting, work

▼ **Fig. 89** is a sketch of the seafront at Sidmouth, Devon. I used a 2B pencil on cartridge drawing paper measuring 20 x 29 cm (8 x 11½ in) and was pleased with the composition of this picture; it looks busy and I like the silhouette of the fishing boat on the left

SIDMOUTH BEACH 24 AUG 83

hard at it and master it. When the time comes to sell your work, remember it's the public that will buy your work and through them that you will earn a living; so be prepared to listen to them. Their comments – good or bad – can be of immense value.

Early in your career (perhaps later on you will have to be a little selective) don't be too proud to accept unusual commissions. You'll benefit from the experience. I once painted two fascia boards for a butcher's shop with pigs, sheep and cows.

A number of years ago I appeared on a live phone-in radio broadcast. In summing up at the end of the programme the presenter said to me: 'Would you say that the most important asset of a successful artist is a natural talent?' 'No, it isn't,' I replied. It was not the answer she was expecting. Obviously taken aback and concerned that the programme time was running out, she asked: 'What is it then?' 'The will to want to get on,' I replied.

Those were my closing words to the first edition of this book, ten years ago but the passage of time hasn't changed my mind at all. When you are painting you sometimes reach a point where your painting doesn't seem to be working out and you need all your willpower and experience to paint through that barrier. Making a success of a career is very similar. I know that if I hadn't had the willpower to work through disappointments, the next ten years could have been very different.

Private collection

▲ **Fig. 90** *After the Storm*, 41 x 61 cm (16 x 24 in), was painted in acrylics during one of those long spells of rain we seem to get in England, where everywhere you go it's 'welly weather'. I do like painting scenes like this and I especially love muddy paths, with lots of puddles. In fact, most of my winter landscapes have puddles in them. I used only five colours throughout the painting and these were Coeruleum Blue, Crimson, Raw Umber, Bright Green, Cadmium Yellow and White

Figs. 91 and 92: Author's collection, Fig. 93: Private collection

▲ Fig. 91

▼ Fig. 92   ▲ Fig. 93

Fig. 91 *Ilkley from the Moors*, 25 x 30 cm (10 x 12 in), oil on primed hardboard, was painted after driving to Yorkshire for the British Watercolour Society Annual Exhibition in 1993. It was late evening and all the colours and tones were soft and indistinct. It took an hour, and I enjoyed every minute of it. The long journey must have inspired me!

Fig. 92 is a watercolour, 38 x 51 cm (15 x 20 in), that I painted late one evening at Porthleven, Cornwall. With only an hour to go before dark, I worked quickly wet-on-wet, then left it to dry before adding more washes to give shape and form. Then, in the last few minutes of daylight, I went over the painting with a felt-tip pen to give shape and form to the rocks. This type of quick watercolour, painted under pressure, doesn't always succeed – I was lucky with this one

Fig. 93 *Summer* is a detail from an acrylic painting, 51 x 76 cm (20 x 30 in). This takes me back to my early childhood. When I am working on a painting like this I get completely lost in the past and relive those happy early years

Chapter 6

FIRST BRUSHES WITH FILMING

T he next ten years were very hectic. Although the majority of my time at the beginning of this period was spent painting for galleries and exhibitions, a subtle change was taking place.

With the success of my books and the Salston courses, I realized just how many people wanted to be helped to paint. Naturally, these people were of all ages and abilities but the majority were either retired or had a strong desire to paint as a hobby. The one thing that they all had in common was that they didn't have the opportunity or, more importantly, the time to engage in a full-time academic course at a school of art. My teaching methods were directed towards this vast and dedicated group of students. Consequently, I found that a lot of my time and energy was being spent in teaching through my books and painting courses.

In 1985, an idea I had been turning over in my mind began to excite me more and more. This new venture was to make an instructional teaching video on painting in watercolour. This may not seem particularly innovative today but, in the mid-eighties,

▲ I had been invited to demonstrate and lecture for the South Wales Art Society's centenary in 1987 at the Reardon Smith Lecture Theatre in Cardiff. June and I had a wonderful time. However, here I look as if I am trying to hypnotize the painting – or to make it disappear!

▲ Here I am doing a book-signing in the Arts and Graphics of Redruth bookshop in Cornwall in 1986. This was followed by a demonstration to a packed house which was organized by the shop. I do enjoy giving demonstrations – it is great to get direct feedback from students

there were no instructional painting videos on the market. However, before even thinking about the content of the video, there were two hurdles to overcome. The first was the finance and the second (and most daunting) was the marketing and distribution. In those days, video shops were few and far between and they were definitely not interested in selling art instructional videos! The only solution was to sell the video by mail order and, in order to do this, we would have to create a small marketing company. It took many months before the pieces fell into place. Two good friends, who would work in their spare time, joined June and myself, and our marketing company Teaching Art was formed.

By now June and I had found out the approximate cost of making an hour-long video. It was expensive but we decided to invest our money in the project. Now all we had to do was actually make the video!

Not surprisingly, our video venture became the most demanding aspect of our daily lives, although it still had to fit in with all our other activities. The biggest problem was deciding on a format. We couldn't look critically at other art videos on the market. As I have said before, none existed, so we were completely on our own. If our video flopped, a tremendous amount of time, energy and money would have been spent and our enthusiasm for trying another way forward into teaching art would have been considerably dampened. A great deal was at stake! June and I finally decided that I should follow the pattern that had proved so successful in my art instruction books, since this was my natural way of teaching.

Our next step was to hire a video production company and for four hectic days my painting studio in Ottery St Mary was transformed into a film set. Six agonizing weeks later, after editing, we saw the finished video and were thrilled with the result.

My video *Learn to Paint with Watercolour* was launched with a full page advertisement in the May 1986 issue of *Leisure Painter* magazine and, at the same time, we launched

◀ With guests at the opening of my joint exhibition with June and our daughter Donna at the Godalming Galleries in Surrey. June is second from the right and Donna is third from the right in the photograph

a new club called *Alwyn's Artists*. Everybody who bought a video was eligible for free membership and our aim was to bring leisure painters together and keep them informed about what was going on in the amateur art world with a twice-yearly newsletter.

The video started to sell – slowly at first, simply because the majority of the people in the market that we were aiming at didn't have video machines in 1986! We were thrilled to get a review in the *Times Educational Supplement* and even more delighted that it was a favourable one. After ten years, this is still one of my best-selling videos. It has been translated into French, German and Dutch and has sold in over fifteen different countries.

It took approximately eighteen months from the concept of the video to its launch

and, during this time, we had plenty of other activities to keep us busy. In 1985, June and I had an exhibition with our youngest daughter, Donna, at her husband Andrew's gallery in Surrey. This was a great success and the three of us went on the radio to talk about the exhibition. This was both June and Donna's first radio interview and they were understandably nervous but they came over like true professionals.

I remember one particular radio programme that rattled my nerves more than a little! I had been invited to do a live 'phone-in' for the BBC in Devon. This meant that I would be in the studio with the presenter while listeners phoned in to ask questions about painting. Although I enjoy this type of programme, you always have to be on your toes because anything can happen when you are on the air. The programme was to go out live at 9 a.m. from their Plymouth studios, so June and I set off early with plenty of time to spare. However, because conditions were terrible, with heavy rain and gale-force winds and slow-moving traffic, our hour-long journey took nearly twice that.

We arrived at the studios with six minutes to spare and my state of panic increased when we found the building looking completely deserted! Through the locked glass doors, I spotted a woman cleaning and persuaded her to let us in. The last four minutes before we went on air were indescribable. An unlit, unmanned studio was quickly brought to life by a technician, I sat in front of a microphone and put on a set of earphones and, before I had a proper chance to adjust them or get comfortable, a loud voice in my ear said, 'And my guest this morning is Alwyn Crawshaw!' With my heart pounding and my mind racing, I listened as another voice asked the first question.

An added difficulty was that, as we were having a three-way conversation from totally different locations in Devon, we couldn't see each other's reactions to the conversation. When a radio presenter is with you, you can help each other with timing, or a difficult listener, by using hand signals and facial expressions – but not today! I can't remember what that first question was, or how I answered it, but luckily I quickly settled down and the programme was a success. Afterwards, I was told, with many

apologies, that we had been sent to the wrong studio – it should have been their other one which was in Exeter, just twenty minutes' drive from our home!

I had another close shave when I needed to be in Leicester to record a programme for BBC Radio. June and I were to travel from Devon by a direct train that would get us there over two hours before the programme was due to go out live. Unfortunately, there had been flooding overnight in most parts of the country and, after many hold-ups, our train was terminated just a few miles from where we had started our journey. We then had to travel by coach, three different trains

and a taxi, finally arriving at the radio station nearly seven hours later, wet and weary with two minutes to spare. Fortunately, times like these are exceptions rather than the rule!

In 1986, Harrods invited me to hold another exhibition and June and I decided to make it a joint exhibition. Sadly, although it was one of the most successful exhibitions I ever held there, it was to be the last one. At the time, the Harrods picture gallery was in the process of changing its image. Ironically, it has now turned full circle and is very similar to how it was before. I didn't hold another exhibition for three years. This was a

Figs. 94 and **95**

Although I love steam trains, I hadn't painted one since *Minnie*, six years earlier (see page 55). Only fifteen minutes' walk from where we lived at Ottery St Mary were the remains of an old branch line of the Great Western Railway. The track had been pulled up in the 1960s and the station was now someone's house. I decided to reconstruct scenes of trains in this area for our Godalming exhibition. Local people were very helpful and eventually I gathered enough information to work from. I then found locations on the old track and did some pencil sketches. Five Arches, the bridge in the second painting, now serves as a path for cows to cross the river. I don't know what they did when the trains were running there!

▲ Fig. 94   ▼ Fig. 95

Figs. 94 and 95 are in private collections

shared one with June at the Patricia Wells Gallery in Bristol. However, this gave me more time for progressing my other commitments. My art instruction books were selling so well that I was now writing one each year. In fact, since writing my first book in 1979, I have now written 20 books, all published by HarperCollins. One of them, *A Brush with Art*, was in the Best-Seller List for six consecutive weeks. This was the first time that an art instruction book had ever been in that list.

I must confess that I am thrilled by the success of my books and the faith that my publisher has had in my work. I have sold nearly two million books worldwide and a statistic that I find particularly rewarding is that one of my books is taken out of a public library in the UK every two minutes.

Writing books has now become a way of life with me and they give me tremendous satisfaction. Perhaps one of the most exciting moments of my life was when June and I recently visited the book section of the National Gallery in London and I saw my books on the shelves. My mind flew back to the times when, as a teenager, I used to visit the gallery and gaze in awe at the Constable paintings before rushing home to pick up my own paint brush. Now my art books are on sale in the same building!

During this period and up to 1988, I was also busy researching the possibility of teaching painting on television. I think I have probably used up more nervous energy on this project over the years than anything else! There were plenty of false starts, including several broken promises from different independent television production companies, who would initially agree to make a pilot film. Each time, this would put me into a state of almost uncontrollable excitement. However, months later, after successive meetings had put the project on hold for a while longer, the inevitable always seemed to happen. The idea would be cancelled and for days I would plunge headlong into despair.

One company kept me 'dangling' for over two years. It was going to happen, then it wasn't, then it was revived, then it wasn't, and so on. This entailed many meetings at my home and in London. The last meeting, at my studio in Devon, was a good one. The producer spent a day with me working out

the filming sequences. At last everything was arranged and a date was fixed for the crew to start filming. The day before filming (with all my normal work having been rescheduled), I telephoned the production company. Call it sixth sense, but I had an uneasy feeling. I was met with the words, 'Didn't you get my letter? We cancelled it because a bigger production turned up'. Total despair again!

The furthest we got at that time was with a company who spent a whole week filming. Ten weeks later, they presented us with four minutes of film – and then decided not to go any further! After six years of playing this emotional game of snakes and ladders, I was adamant. It was time to give up thoughts of television – for the present anyway! As a result, life became easier, with more time for painting, writing books, demonstrating and exhibitions. Then I met David...

Late one afternoon in September 1989, I had an excited telephone call from John Hope-Hawkins, my friend and partner in Teaching Art. He told me that a producer called David John Hare had been trying to contact me with the possibility of making a television series on painting. John hadn't realized how serious I was when I had said, 'no more television', and spent the next hour trying to persuade me just to talk to David. In the end, I agreed, although I was reluctant to play the game of snakes and ladders again.

David turned out to be a very likeable and persuasive young man, who certainly knew how to get my adrenalin and excitement going. After quarter of an hour on the telephone, I was right back to square one, excitedly explaining to him how I saw the format of a television series. June gave me a knowing look, which plainly said, 'here we go again'!

David made promises just like the other producers, but he kept every single one of them. So at last I was on the television ladder. It certainly changed our pattern of life. We made the first series *A Brush with Art* early in 1990 and we have made a series each year since then. I have also written a book to accompany each television series and together this takes about three months to do. This has meant losing three months out of my normal working year, or finding three months extra. I really can't work out what the compromise has been because I still seem to do everything!

▶ A dream come true. My first television series *A Brush with Art* was made in 1990 and I was delighted when my tie-in book to the series entered the Bestseller List and stayed there for six consecutive weeks – a first for an art instruction book!

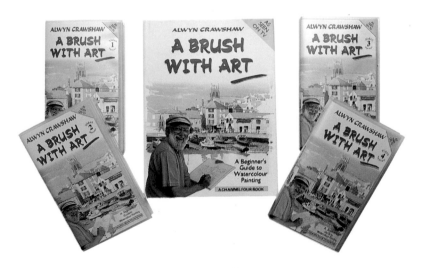

▶ **Fig. 96** *Steady, Ben – we're not off yet!* Acrylic on canvas, 75 x 100 cm (30 x 40 in). This painting was done for the last exhibition I held at Harrods in 1986. I worked from a pencil sketch and memory. I find that a pencil sketch, drawn from nature, is enough for me to work from for this type of landscape. However, I must stress that memory can only be fed by observation. I can only remember different seasonal conditions and colours because these are stored in my head from countless hours of observation and painting practice outdoors

Private collection

A Thrilling Commission

I was commissioned in 1986 to paint a picture for the 5th Royal Inniskilling Dragoon Guards (Royal Dragoon Guards) 'D' Squadron. They had been the Demonstration Tank Squadron at the School of Infantry at Warminster for two years, and the painting was to commemorate their two-year duty. This was organized by a good friend of mine, Major Michael Dover, who was a member of the Regiment.

A date was made for me to go to the squadron's headquarters to do some preliminary sketching and meet the Squadron Leader, Major David Montgomery. When I arrived, I was met with a hive of activity. The the squadron had returned early that morning from the firing ranges at Lulworth, Dorset, and all the tanks were in the hangars being overhauled and cleaned up in preparation for an inspection later.

The ground was covered with engine parts, tool boxes, spares of all descriptions, cleaning equipment and pots of paint. All the time, there was the continuous throb of engines, the harsh sound of metal banging against metal and the shouts and curses of the crews as they worked hard on their machines. Added to that, every so often, the busy scene would disappear from view in clouds of diesel exhaust, as engines were revved into life.

After taking me inside the comparative quiet of a tank and showing me some of its operating parts, Major Montgomery gave his blessing to wander around and sketch at will. By this time, my artistic adrenalin was flowing madly and my excitement level was nearly off the Richter scale!

I made my way carefully around the tanks, observing and soaking up this tremendously exciting atmosphere and chatting to some of the soldiers. Then I decided it was time to do my first sketch of a tank. The result was terrible! The reason was simple; I was too excited about the situation and I hadn't given myself a chance to wind down. I moved away from the hangars, sat down on my sketching stool and said to myself: 'Relax, Alwyn – you're a professional and you have a job of work to do!' Ten minutes later, I was back sketching the same tank and this time I was happy with the result (see Fig. 97). I was now relaxed and enjoying my sketching. As I

◄ **Fig. 97** My second preliminary sketch of the tank, after the first one had been a disaster! 2B pencil on cartridge paper, 15 x 45 cm (6 x 18 in)

worked, a lot of noise was coming from a tank a little way to my left. The crew were trying to start the engine but were having little success. Eventually, enshrouded by a larger than normal cloud of exhaust, the tank started up and very slowly rumbled towards me. It felt as though the ground was moving beneath my feet as it passed by, at the same time, completely covering both me and my sketchpad with a shower of black diesel soot! Fortunately, when I arrived, I had been given army overalls to wear.

I quickly turned around to look at the tank, which was now about three metres (nine feet) away from me and suddenly it blew up! Flames shot high into the air from the engine compartment at the rear of the tank and I could feel the heat from where I stood. Within seconds, soldiers were running to the scene, while others jumped from their tanks, and, all brandishing fire extinguishers, converged on the stricken tank.

Eventually the fire was put out and I tried to carry on sketching, but it wasn't easy! Fortunately, soon after this, I was taken to lunch and this gave me time to relax again. But word had gone around that the incident had happened where 'the artist' was sketching. This became a big joke with Michael and Major Montgomery – after all, incidents like that don't happen every day!

During the afternoon, I did some more information sketches and was taken up to the ranges, where we eventually found a good painting location. A day was arranged for me

Author's collection

◀ **Fig. 98** I painted this watercolour of the tank on Whatman 200lb Not, 38 x 50 cm (15 x 20 in), on my second visit as a preliminary to the commissioned painting, which would be worked in acrylics back home. I had already done information sketches and taken photographs to work from. The object of this painting was simply to experience capturing the scene with paint

to go back and work on a watercolour of the proposed painting at this location.

I returned a couple of weeks later and was thrilled to be invited to ride the twenty-minute journey to the ranges in the tank that I would paint. It was a marvellous experience, standing in the turret with the tank commander. Unfortunately, it was a grey, overcast day, with wind and drizzling rain, but this had been anticipated and a four-ton covered lorry came along with us. I would work from the back of this vehicle, out of the rain.

Sadly, the plan wasn't watertight! When I got into the back of the lorry to do my watercolour, the open end was facing the oncoming elements. Consequently, I had to

go further inside to avoid the wind and driving rain and, naturally, the further I retreated, the darker it became. So I did the watercolour (Fig. 98) dodging most of the rain, but in very difficult light conditions.

I was wet, my hands were extremely cold, it was difficult to see the tank and almost impossible to see the colours I was mixing, but I thoroughly enjoyed the experience.

Michael arrived on the scene while I was painting and, when I had finished, asked me if I would like to drive the tank. My thoughts went back to my first visit and the exploding engine but then adult caution was thrown to the wind and I heard myself saying, 'yes, please', like an excited schoolboy. I was shown how to get into the driver's seat, which in itself was no mean feat. I was then shown how to drive it by a crew member, who crouched on the tank at the side of me (see the photograph, right).

When I was finally given a helmet and earphones and told to start the engine, the thrill was enormous. My foot trembled on the accelerator pedal but, as I gained confidence, I put pressure on and slowly we moved forward. From my small, confined space at the very front, it was hard to believe I was actually driving a 55-ton tank! The commander was in the turret all the time, keeping a watchful eye on events and communicating with the instructor.

We did a very wide circle around the lorry where Michael and Major Montgomery were having a chat and keeping a watchful eye on me. I must say that descending a steep crater wall was a little unnerving, but when we got back to the our starting point again, my instructor said, 'Okay, you've got the idea now. Let's go again, but this time put your foot down!'.

So off the tank went again, with a very excited artist at the controls! I had been experiencing difficulty in pulling the two 'levers' that steer the tank and had found one in particular very hard to shift. I had told my instructor this during our first drive, but since his answer was, 'If you pull it harder, it will work', I had decided that I simply wasn't as strong as these young soldiers.

Now I was heading straight at the lorry with my two-man audience standing by it. I

◀ I think I resemble a little gnome here, with my head sticking out of the tank, as I listen carefully to my driving instructor. This was before my great adventure, when I drove the tank single-handed!

was fighting to pull the lever and turn the tank, but it just wouldn't move. At the same time, my instructor was shouting in my earphones for me to pull harder but it was no good. So. in the nick of time, I slammed on the brake and the tank stopped dead in front of the lorry.

As it stopped, my instructor whipped off his helmet, got to his feet and disappeared from my view over the tank towards the back. I don't think I've ever seen anybody move so fast! I sat there wondering what was going on for about twenty seconds, then he came clattering back, yelling, 'Out, we're on fire!' and then dashed off again.

I must have made a record escape out of that confined compartment! Apart from bruises I got when I hit parts of the tank as I scrambled up through the small hatch, I was fine. The fire was eventually put out and I was told it was something to do with the steering brakes. The reason why I couldn't

pull the levers to manoeuver the tank was now satisfactorily explained – it wasn't due to weakness or old age!

Incidentally, during my first visit, Michael had asked me if I would like to paint helicopters at the Army helicopter base, saying that he would organize a flight in one and perhaps my painting could depict a scene from a flying helicopter. However, after the two tank incidents where 'the artist' happened to be in such close proximity, he hasn't mentioned the matter again – and I haven't prompted him!

The following week I worked at home from my information sketches, the watercolour painting, the photographs I had taken and my memory, and painted three pictures; two in acrylics and one in oils. The specific one I did for the commission (Fig. 99) was also made into a limited edition fine art print for the members of the regiment. Time permitting, I would love some more commissions like this.

By kind permision of the 5th Royal Inniskilling Dragoon Guards

▲ **Fig. 99** The commissioned painting was worked in acrylics on canvas, 50 x 75 cm (20 x 30 in). This was done after two days of intensive involvement with tanks and their crews, pencil sketching for atmosphere and detail, and a watercolour painting. I would not have attempted a painting like this without such preliminary work since it is important to be familiar with your subject to obtain the best results.

I drew the tank very carefully in pencil first. Next I painted in the sky and trees and then worked on the tank until I was happy with its shape and form (without detail). The next step was to paint in the foreground. The canvas was now covered and, after some modification, I worked in the detail of the tank and its surroundings

Chapter 7

EXCITING NEW VENTURES

We had now been living in Devon for nine years. Our house at Ottery St Mary was not remote, but you definitely needed instructions to find us. Even so, over the years, many of my students and people who had read my books found me and asked if they could see my studio. Naturally, we were not organized for the public but I never turned anyone away and always found time to talk to them.

One of our ambitions had always been to have our own gallery. Then students would be able to find us easily and June and I would have a permanent exhibition of our work on show. For the last two years, we had been searching for the right place and eventually, in 1989, we finally found Lammas Park House, a Georgian building in the seaside town of Dawlish, just twenty miles away. The property had been a hotel and, although it provided adequate space for a home, studios for both June and myself and a gallery, it needed a great deal of renovation. This was done by builders while we were living in situ, and I wouldn't recommend this to anyone!

Author's collection

◀ **Fig. 100** I did this watercolour sketch of our house and gallery in my A4 size sketchbook. I was sitting amongst builder's rubble at the time, trying to forget what we were living through while the property was being renovated!

However, after six months of plaster dust, dirt and total discomfort, the builders finally finished and we had our own gallery and studios with very comfortable living accommodation. Dawlish even has an express train service direct to London and this has been a tremendous bonus.

During this upheaval, our normal working life continued. I was writing another book, *Alwyn Crawshaw's Watercolour Painting Course*, and both June and I were painting for the autumn exhibition to be held at the Patricia Wells Gallery at Thornbury, Bristol, in October 1989. We had now taken our last painting course at the Salston Hotel. Sadly, it had been sold and the new owners weren't interested in running painting courses. However, we didn't stay idle!

In the past, we had been invited by the *Leisure Painter* magazine to take painting courses abroad under their banner but had always declined since we couldn't spare the time and I didn't like flying. Now we had some time to spare, I conquered my fear of flying and we took our first painting course abroad. We went to Provence, in France, with twenty adult students.

During 1990, as well as moving home, our three major activities: television, teaching abroad and running a gallery, were all new adventures. To pack them all into one year, along with our normal workload, was perhaps a little ambitious. But you can't always arrange events in life to neatly fit into place when you want them to. For me, the old saying, 'all or nothing' is very true!

I am also a firm believer that when you want to start something new, talking about it is very important. But the most important aspect of all is to discuss the position you will be in if it fails. At this time, June and I appreciated that we were taking risks in order to achieve our dreams. For instance, if our gallery failed, we would be living in a house far too big for us and might have to sell our new home and move again. Naturally, we would have also failed in one of our ambitions and would have to live with that disappointment. But we work as a team and

◀ Our first painting course in France was very exciting. We found the Provençal countryside very inspiring – I think a few other artists before us have felt the same way! But why is it that when I am totally involved in a demonstration for students, it has to rain? Here I am packing up my oil pochade box. (I'm glad to see that the students look happy, despite the weather!)

were both prepared to accept the realities of failure if we didn't succeed.

The opening day of the gallery was a tremendous success. We had decided it would be a family gallery and we would also hang the work of our two daughters, Donna and Natalie, my twin sister Shirley and my younger sister, Pam, who are all artists. It was a very exciting day for all of us. The gallery was packed to capacity and we had visitors from as far afield as Manchester, Birmingham, London and Essex.

Naturally, June and I aren't able to be in the gallery every day and we are very fortunate to employ Mary Poole, who has looked after the running of it since it opened. Although Mary works in the environment of

painting and has my videos running constantly in the gallery, I have yet to persuade her to take up a paintbrush and have a go. Still you can't win them all!

My biggest – and most nerve-racking – adventure in 1990 was filming my first television series, *A Brush with Art*. Since I was to paint 'live' on camera for each programme, if anything went wrong it would mean starting the painting again from the beginning. I knew that a lot depended on me – if I ruined a picture, it could mean another day's work and totally rearranging the complex filming schedules for other days – not to mention extra cost!

For one programme, it had been decided that I would sit outside a harbourside café in

Polperro and paint the view, and this had been pre-arranged with the proprietor. However, on the day, it was raining so heavily that filming outside was out of the question. Rather than lose time, a new programme was quickly devised by David, our director Ingrid, June and myself at eight o'clock that morning. Then, after nearly four hours of searching and negotiating in the monsoon-type weather, I finished up in a fisherman's hut doing a pen and wash

Author's collection

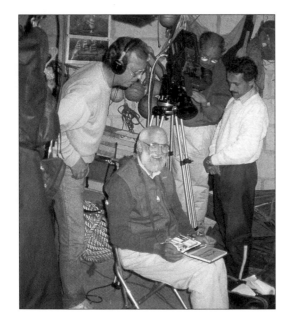

▲ After hours of rain-swept negotiations and replanning, the show went on in the fisherman's hut. (It was actually one of the most successful programmes of that series!)

▲ **Fig. 101** is the pen and wash painting I did from the fisherman's hut for television. I used a 2B pencil on Ivorex board, 28 x 39 cm (11 x 15 in), then painted very freely with watercolour. Finally, I used a 'dip in' pen and Indian ink to finish the painting

▶ During a sunnier break in filming for *A Brush with Art*, I show my grandson Russell a painting I have been working on. I look rather worried but, judging by Russell's expression, I think I may have got quite a few marks out of ten this time!

painting of the wind and rainswept harbour. This turned out to be a great success but, as you can imagine, the pressure on me to do a perfect painting first time was very great! So far I have always managed to do this and I have made 52 programmes to date. Thank you, lady luck! Mind you, I can remember one or two close encounters with disaster when I have had to reach deep down into my professional knowledge and experience to pull a painting round!

Near the end of filming for the first television series, we were on the beach at Shaldon in Devon. By the time the crew were set up and ready to film me, a sea mist had come down and I couldn't see the scene I was ready to paint and discuss. Rather than lose a day's filming, June and I sat on the beach and quickly worked out another format for the programme. David was very proud of us, particularly as it could be filmed from the same spot!

Early in 1990, June and I were invited to go to the Cannes Film Festival to help to promote the television series. This was a wonderful experience. We were the guests of TSW (Television South West), the company who had commissioned the series, and our two-day visit was a social whirl of wining and dining, which finished with a cocktail party on board the TSW yacht.

It had been decided that I would sit on deck and paint the view of the harbour while the VIP guests (television executives from around the world) talked to me and discussed

▶ Here I am in Cannes on the TSW yacht painting a scene of the harbour in watercolour. The television crew were making a short clip of me working to be shown on a weekly television programme in England

▶ June and I will never forget that trip to Cannes. Although there was a lot of hectic rushing around to meet different people and talk about the new television series, we still had time to sit in the sun and enjoy ourselves

my painting programmes. I was also filmed and interviewed while I worked for a piece in a weekly British television programme, but to my knowledge this has never been shown.

Back from the excitement and glamour of Cannes, June and I moved on to our next project. We had decided to hold a summer exhibition of paintings of Dartmoor in the gallery and had started painting for this in the previous year. During January and February 1990, we had gone out on Dartmoor in dramatic weather conditions – dark, cloudy skies, wind, rain and sleet – and painted from the comparative comfort of our car. That winter, we certainly felt we had captured some of Dartmoor's best-known moods on paper!

It was only a few weeks after these wild and windy painting trips that we went to Cannes, which provided a complete contrast. But as soon as we were back, we went out on the moors again. Now spring was in the air and we were able to capture Dartmoor in another of its wonderful moods.

During the previous year, another of my books, *The Half-Hour Painter*, was published. Inspired by the New Year's resolution I made – and broke – back in 1983

Private collection

▲ **Fig. 102** *The Warren House Inn, Dartmoor.* Watercolour on cartridge paper, 20 x 28 cm (8 x 11 in). I did this sketch on one of our winter trips to Dartmoor, from inside the car. On that occasion, it rained all day! I find it reasonably comfortable to work in the car although, naturally, you can't paint large sizes. I have done paintings 38 x 50 cm (15 x 20 in) in the car, although it did get a little cramped!

Private collection

▲ **Fig. 103** *Evening Shadows at Hound Tor, Dartmoor.* Watercolour on Bockingford 200 lb, 25 x 38 cm (10 x 15 in). This is one of June's paintings from a Dartmoor trip. She was inspired by the strong sunlight and shadows on the rocks. The best light for painting is in the early morning or late evening when shadows are long, as they help to give shape and form. Around midday a landscape can look very flat and uninteresting. June certainly saw this scene at the right time (see page 64), the purpose of this book was to encourage students to paint a picture in just half an hour. This is a good way to learn how to observe and to simplify whatever you are painting. It doesn't matter what the painting looks like, the object is to learn from doing the exercise. It also helps the student to gain self-discipline and not to overwork a painting – or fiddle!

The book was a great success and is now in its seventh reprint. Back in March 1990, BBC's *Daytime Live* invited me to take part in their programme and to paint a picture live on television in half an hour.

June and I arrived early at the Pebble Mill studios in Birmingham on the day of the programme and, after discussion with the producer and the presenter, Judy Spiers, a painting spot was chosen outside in the studio gardens. These were full of daffodils and looked wonderful on camera but I knew this wasn't really my type of subject. However, I had agreed to paint it – and in just half an hour!

If you happened to see that programme from the comfort of your home, I can let you into a secret – it was bitterly cold! In fact, I was issued with 'body warmers' to place on various parts of my anatomy, although the viewers couldn't see them.

I was introduced at the beginning of the programme by Judy and then left outside in the garden to paint the picture, while the programme continued live inside the studio. Now the cameras, sound equipment and

◀ Alone amongst the daffodils with no way out. The *Daytime Live* television programme was well under way and I had claimed, in front of millions of viewers, that I could paint this scene in half an hour. There was no turning back!

television crew had gone, June and I were out there all alone, but totally committed. After all, even as we sat there, the programme was going out to millions of homes around the country, with the viewers waiting to see the results of my painting.

I looked at the blank piece of paper on my knees and suddenly realized just what I had let myself in for. It was a very frightening moment! But, although it felt like hours, it was actually just a few moments before I got down to the job in hand.

In the final four minutes, while I was putting some last, but very important, washes on the painting, I dropped my brush in the dirt. I couldn't retrieve it because it was out of my reach but June quickly saw my dilemma. She came rushing over, picked up the brush and quickly washed it in a stream that runs through the garden. If she

had dipped it in my water jar, it would have turned the contents to mud! I was then able to finish the painting. Seconds later, the camera crew, carrying their equipment, came hurrying back and Judy held my wet painting up to the camera to show the viewers the result of my half-hour's work. Despite having been half-frozen while I did the painting (not to mention under tremendous pressure!), I was rather pleased with the result.

Off the air, Judy said she was surprised that I hadn't done another painting of the scene before the programme started, just in case I had problems with the one I did 'live'. I said this would never have occurred to me. After all, if I had produced a complete disaster, I would have still shown it to the viewers and simply explained what had gone wrong with it.

Author's collection

▲ Fig. 104 I did this sketch as a demonstration for the students on our trip to Tuscany. A few of them were against my putting the car into the painting but, once it was finished, they agreed it looked correct. When painting from nature, within reason, I paint what I see

▶ The students moved away while June took this photograph of me working on the street scene in the painting shown above. It was a glorious day – for once I was blessed with sunny weather for my painting demonstration!

In the summer of 1991, we took students on a painting course to Tuscany. The warm Italian earth colours, ranging from golden yellows to deep reddy-browns, were breathtaking and very inspiring. Incidentally, a frustrating aspect of teaching art is that, while you are enthusing about your surroundings and motivating your students, you don't have much time to do any serious painting yourself.

I always do some demonstrations for my students, so my brush isn't totally idle, and Fig. 104 (left) is a sketch that I did on that trip to Tuscany. But, each time June and I come back from taking a painting course abroad, we always say that we will return to do some painting purely for pleasure. And then, of course, we never find the time!

Before we went to Tuscany, we made my second television series, *Crawshaw Paints Oils*, in Devon. We had our usual location problems while filming, and there was one incident in particular that I certainly won't forget in a hurry.

I was painting the Exe Estuary from a hill and we were in a clearing surrounded by fir trees. There was just enough room for the crew, cameras and my easel.

We spent the whole morning taking establishing shots of me arriving on the scene, telling the viewers where we were and what I was going to paint. I had also been filmed drawing the scene ready for painting. Then we packed up the equipment and went for lunch.

Although we were miles from anywhere and there was no-one else in sight, I made the observation to David that, by the time we returned, someone else might be on our painting spot. He said, 'Alwyn, you worry too much!'.

Well, it must have been my sixth sense again because, when we returned from lunch, we saw a solitary car parked near to the fir trees. David carefully avoided eye contact with me as we neared our clearing and came upon an elderly couple sitting on chairs next to a Primus stove with a kettle simmering away – almost exactly on my painting spot.

David politely explained our filming dilemma and asked them if they would be willing to let us move their 'camp' for them. However, they simply wouldn't budge. We had no option but to carry on filming around them, making sure we did not get them in the shot. It was also a little distracting for me because I had to paint and talk to the camera while the couple had their picnic almost on top of me!

Finally, to make matters worse, a heavy mist came down and I had a real fight against time to finish the painting as the scene in front of me gradually disappeared from view! At the end of that day, I think the whole crew must have shared my feelings of 'only just made it!'.

During 1991, Daler-Rowney stopped sponsoring artists to demonstrate at local art societies. Instead, they devised a format of

▶ **Fig. 105** *Cricket Match, Ottery St Mary, Devon.* Primed canvas, 40 x 60 cm (16 x 24 in). This is one of the paintings I did under camera for the television series *Crawshaw Paints Oils.* It was a very hot day – fortunately I was in the shade! I was reasonably happy with the painting but the shadow in the foreground is much too brown and has always annoyed me. Still, you can't win them all!

Author's collection

▶ Here I am in full swing at the Norwich Roadshow, which was a great success. June and I have found that, whichever part of the country we visit, the warmth and enthusiasm shown by the audiences at our roadshows is quite overwhelming and makes all the hard work and preparation more than worthwhile

'painting roadshows' and started putting these on around the country. The venues are usually large lecture halls with space for an audience of two or three hundred people. A video camera films the painting as it is being done and this is shown on a big screen so everyone in the audience gets a good view. This is a wonderful way of seeing a painting being done 'live' by the artist. In fact, it's very interesting for me, too, as it enables me to see what I am doing in fantastic detail.

After our gruelling train journey to Leicester (see page 96), I was due to do a roadshow at the Leicester University the following day. Once I had finished the BBC broadcast, June and I went straight to our hotel to meet members of the Daler-Rowney team, discuss ideas, have a bite to eat and get some much-needed sleep!

By nine o'clock the next morning, I was already busy on stage at the university, liaising with the camera man and setting up my painting equipment in preparation for that afternoon's event.

That day we also had a very important lunch date in Leicester. This was with the winners of a children's painting competition which June and I had judged earlier in the year for the National Federation of Families with Visually Impaired Children. We presented the prizes and had a chance to talk to these remarkable children.

Then it was back to the lecture theatre, where people were already gathering for the roadshow. For the next forty-five minutes, I signed books and June and I talked to members of the audience. Then for the next two-and-a-half hours I painted a watercolour from beginning to end, while talking and answering questions continuously. Even in the half-hour break during the show and at the end of it, I still continued to sign books and talk. I'm surprised I didn't lose my voice!

Then it was time to tidy up and prepare for the evening show, which was a virtual repeat of my afternoon's performance. By the time June and I got back to our hotel, close to midnight, we were more than ready to fall into our beds!

The following morning we were up early and travelled to Nottingham where I went on another BBC radio show, followed by a two-hour book signing session in one of the city's book shops and finally June and I caught the train home, thankfully this time with no mishaps! It's amazing what you can pack into two days. Mind you, you could do with two days' rest to get over it, although you never seem to find them!

It is always rewarding to help other artists along the road to success and a most enjoyable activity over the years has been my involvement with new art societies – professional and non-professional.

Having been invited to join the Society of Equestrian Artists back in 1979 when it was just a year old, I was a member of their council for the first five years, often travelling to London for meetings and lively discussions about the future of the society. I was also thrilled to win the prize for the Best Watercolour at their Annual Exhibition on four occasions.

The National Acrylic Painters Association, based in Liverpool, was founded by Kenneth Hodgson in 1985. I was invited to join and, in 1991, became President. We found a permanent home for our annual exhibition in 1993 when the Council of The Royal Birmingham Society of Artists and its President, Ernest Horton, kindly offered us the use of their own gallery in Birmingham.

Another society I belong to is the British Watercolour Society. I am told by its Director, Leslie Simpson, that records go back to 1911 and are vague before that. Since Leslie took over as Director in 1985 the Society has gone from strength to strength and I was delighted when, in 1994, I was invited to become its Vice President.

I have been President of my local amateur society, the Otter Vale Art Society, for the past twelve years. I am also President of the Devon Art Society, which was founded in 1912 by a group of Royal Academicians and has a long and illustrious history. Arthur Hacker RA was its first president and Dame Laura Knight SWA was an early member of this society.

▶ In 1993 I opened the Annual Exhibition of the National Acrylic Painters Association. This was held for the first time at the Royal Birmingham Society of Artists' gallery in Birmingham and was a great success

Author's collection

▲ **Fig. 106**
Self Portrait. Oil on canvas, 30 x 25 cm (12 x 10 in). I don't consider myself to be a portrait painter. In fact, I can count the portraits I have sketched or painted on one hand.

However, during Christmas 1992, for some unknown reason, I had a burning desire to paint a self portrait. After over two hours of very intense but enjoyable painting, I was pleased with the result

In 1991 I was thrilled to learn that the first watercolour video that I made back in 1986 had won acclaim in the USA, and I had been voted one of the 'top ten' video teaching artists for that year in America.

Our painting course that year took us to Greece and we had a wonderful time. By now many of the students had joined us before on other courses, so we were meeting up with old friends as well as making new ones.

In August 1990, I had been interviewed on BBC Radio Devon and Cornwall by John Reynolds. I had been on his programmes many times before and John was always coming up with new ideas. This time he suggested that I did a drawing of him working during one of his broadcasts. I agreed, although I couldn't help remembering that other 'live' show in the deserted studio and made sure that June and I arrived at the correct BBC studio in Exeter this time! John and I had a chat on air first and then I sat in the corner working away. Suddenly, he turned and talked to June, still on air. This took her completely by surprise but, as usual, she handled it like a true professional.

In 1991 we made our third television series, *Crawshaw Paints on Holiday*. This was filmed on the island of Majorca and, although she was very nervous to start with, David and I managed to persude June to appear on television for the first time painting in front of the cameras.

June found it reasonably 'easy' to talk to the camera, but a little more difficult when

▶ **Fig. 107** I did this pencil and watercolour sketch of John Reynolds in half an hour as part of our interview for BBC Radio Devon and Cornwall

By kind permission of BBC Radio Devon

▲ In a holiday mood – until now, only a few people have seen my bare legs! June snapped this on our painting course to Greece in 1991. My pencil sketch of a donkey (right) was done with 2B pencil on cartridge paper

trying to paint and talk at the same time! For her television début, she was going to paint a palm tree (which looked more like a very big pineapple) surrounded by poppies. She sat waiting with her watercolours in the blazing sun for forty minutes while the camera crew set up. When they were finally ready, she looked at her subject again and said, 'I am going to paint this pineapple tree'. Later, June got even more confused and said she was going to paint the poppy trees – meaning the poppies!

I completely sympathized with her – I know how easy it is to get tongue-tied on television! Also, being prepared to start and then having to wait can be the most nerve-racking thing of all when you are filming. Incidentally, those lines of June's were kept in the programme.

At that time, June and I were organizing a joint exhibition to be held at the St. Helier Gallery in Jersey in the autumn of 1992. We made two trips to Jersey during the year to sketch and paint local scenes in preparation for the exhibition but most of the paintings were done in our studios at home.

While we were in Jersey, we fitted in a very successful book-signing session in one of St. Helier's major stores. You never know what to expect at book-signings. In some shops, I have been kept busy autographing dozens of books, while in others I have only been asked to put my signature to a few. Some years ago, a book-signing tour was organized for me by HarperCollins in the

north of England. We went from Dawlish to Manchester, then to Leeds, on to Newcastle and, finally, to York. This was all done in four hectic but enjoyable days, with a full house at every shop. It did get confusing being in a different hotel every night, though! Once, we went down to the restaurant in the evening and found it had gone. It hadn't – we'd just confused this hotel with the one we had left that morning!

Author's collection

▲ **Fig. 108** Watercolour on Bockingford paper, 20 x 28 cm (8 x 11 in). This was June's television painting début – her 'pineapple' tree, which she sketched in Majorca for our third television series *Crawshaw Paints on Holiday*

Chapter 8

A DREAM COMES TRUE

In 1992 my first three television series were screened by PBS television for the first time in America. They have now been shown in many countries worldwide, including Bahrain, Japan, Norway, Singapore, Turkey, and Zimbabwe, and so the idea I first had in 1985 of making a teaching video was catching on more than I had ever dreamed possible! I still get letters from all over the world, where my videos or television series have been shown, and it is very encouraging to realize that I can help people of all nationalities in this way with their painting problems.

One of the major activities of 1992, apart from the Jersey exhibition and writing another book, *Crawshaw's Acrylic Painting Course*, was the rebirth of Alwyn's Artists. If you remember, we had launched this club for leisure painters and sent out a regular newsletter to people who had bought the first video. The club had thrived and by 1992 had 4,000 members. For some time, June and I had shared a dream of helping it grow into a national, or maybe even international, society for amateur artists but, up until then,

all our energies and resources had been taken up with other activities. However, now we felt that the time was right.

Together with John Hope-Hawkins, our partner in the company Teaching Art, we decided that we would widen the appeal of Alwyn's Artists. It would be renamed the Society of Amateur Artists, a title which we

▲ In 1992, we somehow found the time to take a painting course in Spain. In the middle of a demonstration to students, I had my usual shower of rain, but brollies were at hand. Well, they say, 'the rain in Spain...'

felt was simple and to the point. As far as we knew, it would be the first international amateur society for painters. In fact, I can't imagine why it hadn't been done before!

After many meetings and discussions, we prepared a complete and detailed plan for the society. This was presented to my publishers, HarperCollins, in London by June, myself, John Hope-Hawkins, his son Richard Hope-Hawkins, who is also a director of Teaching Art, and Chandy Rodgers, John's daughter, who would become Secretary of the society.

Although I had worked with HarperCollins for many years, I was still very nervous. We were asking them to give us help and sponsorship and, although I knew that the society was a viable project, if we weren't able to convince the team at HarperCollins, all our planning and hard work would be in vain. That may explain why I developed a migraine on the train journey up to London that morning – and I had a jumpy tooth, as well! What a way to start an important meeting, although luckily nobody realized how I felt.

HarperCollins were duly impressed and made some very constructive comments and suggestions. They thought that the society was a sound idea and agreed to help us with the sponsorship we needed to get started. I shall always be grateful to them for their help and support. The Society of Amateur Artists was eventually launched on 30 September 1992 and was a tremendous success. As I am writing now in June 1995, we have over 16,000 members in Britain and fifty-one other countries.

That same year, I was invited to open British Painters '92, an exhibition of paintings sponsored by the *Leisure Painter* magazine and held at the Westminster Galleries in London. I was very flattered and quite nervous, but my opening speech went down well and I quickly relaxed!

As I paint in watercolour, acrylic and oil, I am often asked which medium I prefer to work in. The answer is simple – it is the one I am working in at the time. For instance, while I am painting a watercolour, with its luminosity and glorious 'happy accidents', I can't imagine wanting to push solid, heavy oil colours around a canvas. On the other hand, my brush strokes look so strong and positive when I am working in oil that watercolour seems very wishy-washy by comparison! In a nutshell, whatever medium I am working in gets my total commitment. It is never second-best and the same goes for the subject matter of my painting as well.

When you have been concentrating on working in one medium, it can shake your confidence in your ability to paint with another you have neglected for a while.

Sometimes, if I haven't painted with oils for several months, I begin to wonder if I will remember how to use them even though I have been painting for fifty-three years! When this happens, I set a firm date to begin an oil painting and, even more importantly, start imagining the pleasure of working in that medium. Usually, by the time my oil painting day arrives, I am no longer nervous but filled with excitement and enthusiasm. When I did the oil painting on page 68 on location, I hadn't painted in oil for nearly four months.

Although I work outdoors in all mediums, I approach this type of painting in a completely different way to my studio work. When you are painting outside, there usually isn't time to rethink things once you have started and I believe that splashes of paint, smudges on your work, and even flies sticking to an oil painting, are all part of the excitement of working directly from nature (see Figs. 109–111 on page 118).

I enjoy working in the studio just as much. This gives me plenty of time to think and rethink, and also to work on larger paintings (see Figs 112–114 on page 119). Naturally, the paintings I do outside tend to have more freedom and a 'looser' feel than my more 'considered' studio work. But both have their charms and teach you more about being an artist. I suppose I have the same attitude to where I work as I do to the medium I use. Whatever I am doing, I enjoy it and try to give myself totally to the project.

▶ The only qualification needed to join the Society of Amateur Artists is the desire to paint. Activities include local meetings and events organised by regional co-ordinators and members are kept up-to-date about the latest happenings in the amateur art world through regular issues of *PAINT*, the Society's newsletter

The three paintings on this page were all done outside on location.

Fig. 109 *Near Poundsgate, Dartmoor.* Acrylic on primed Waterford paper, 15 x 20 cm (6 x 8 in). When I saw this scene, I immediately noticed the cool blue colours in the distance, contrasting with the much warmer colours in the foreground. I made sure that I put these different tonal values into the painting, because it helped to give an impression of distance

Fig. 110 *Evening Light, Kingsbridge, Devon.* Oil on primed hardboard, 25 x 30 cm (10 x 12 in). This small painting is one of my all-time favourites. I feel that I managed to capture the afternoon sunlight in the picture without overworking it. On this occasion I wasn't tempted to fiddle!

Fig. 111 *From La Roc Gagiac, Dordogne, France.* Watercolour on cartridge paper, 20 x 28 cm (8 x 11 in). This painting was done very freely as a demonstration for the students when we visited France for a painting course. Notice the dark trees in the foreground of the picture, which help to portray distance against the lighter background

▲ Fig. 110   Private collection

▲ Fig. 109   Private collection

▲ Fig. 111   Author's collection

118

The paintings on this page were all done in the studio.

Fig. 112 *Look, it's there again!* Acrylic on canvas, 50 x 80 cm (20 x 30 in.) This is the type of scene I love painting in acrylics. Although I used sketches and photographs for the horses, the scene was done from my imagination. However, don't forget that your imagination has to be fed as much as possible by sketching from life

Fig. 113 *Low Tide, St Auban, Jersey.* Oil on canvas, 75 x 100 cm (30 x 40 in). I did a watercolour, 38 x 25 cm (25 x 10 in) and pencil sketches of the scene while sitting on the harbour wall, and took some photographs. For this painting, I used thin, watery colours for the underpainting. When this was dry, I worked over it with oil paint

Fig. 114 *They said 'Sunny intervals and dry!'.* Watercolour on Waterford 300 lb Rough, 38 x 50 cm (15 x 20 in). All artists have their favourite paintings. I like this one because of the strength and movement of the man and horses but feel I have still kept the softness and delicacy of watercolour

▲ Fig. 113

Author's collection

▲ Fig. 112

Private collection

▲ Fig. 114

By kind permission of Mr Andy Hucklesley

119

It was during 1993 that June and I made a determined effort to go on a non-working holiday for the first time in over six years. We managed to find a week in the summer and took a cruiser on the Norfolk Broads with my sisters, Shirley and Pam, and Ian, Pam's husband. Needless to say, we all spent the week painting – we happened to have our brushes with us – but June and I had a relaxing and enjoyable break and decided to try to do this every year.

Earlier that Spring, we had filmed our fourth television series, *Crawshaw's Watercolour Studio*. This was done mainly in my studio at home and filming was much easier, as it was done in controlled conditions with no picnickers to contend with!

After filming for two weeks, on the very last day I was putting in the final brush stroke on my last painting, when I suddenly relaxed and lost concentration. I was finishing an acrylic painting and, as I painted in some crows in the sky, I was supposed to take the brush away and finish the programme and the series with a few concluding statements. This was to be ad-libbed as usual, as long as I made the important points, and the first take was fine, except I forgot to say a couple of important things.

By the fifth take, there was no room left in the sky for any more birds! So we started the sequence with the brush simply coming away from the canvas. By the tenth take, I was feeling sick inside. Here I was in my own studio with David, all the crew and June

▶ **Fig. 115** I did this sketch of June as she sat sketching on our Norfolk Broads holiday. I painted it in my A4 cartridge sketchbook from inside the boat. Naturally, it was raining!

Author's collection

willing me on, yet I was unable to memorize and join half a dozen sentences together and make sense. Eventually I got it right and everybody relaxed and had a cup of tea and the series was finished.

The following day, I started writing the tie-in book to the television series, feeling a little battle-fatigued but happy that the filming had gone okay. This was then interrupted by three days in Birmingham for the annual NAPA exhibition, four days of demonstrations at the *Artists and Illustrators'* Art Materials Show in London, and then three days at Art in Action, another big art and craft show at Waterperry House in Oxford. I finished the tie-in book to *Crawshaw's Watercolour Studio* just two

▲ Here I am giving a painting demonstration at the *Artists and*

Illustrators' Art Materials Show in London in 1993

days before we left for our holiday on the Norfolk Broads. It had been a hectic few weeks and so that holiday came at just the right time.

In September 1993, June and I took students for a painting course to the Dordogne in France. With its beautiful scenery and fairytale chateaux, we all agreed that it was a painter's paradise.

This was also the year that we started planning the inaugural exhibition of the Society of Amateur Artists. This was held at the Westminster Galleries in London in the May of 1994.

Since we firmly believed that each of the members should have the chance to exhibit some work, whatever their ability, we decided that there would be no preselection of paintings. We had spaces to hang 800 paintings and, as we had over 1,500 members wishing to exhibit, work had to be accepted on a 'first-come, first-hung' basis. By the opening day, the rooms looked magnificent, offering a true representation of amateur work in many mediums and covering a tremendous range of subject matter and style.

The day of the exhibition started for June and I when we were picked up from our London hotel by a chauffeur-driven car from the BBC and taken to Broadcasting House. This was a little different to our journey through rainstorms to Plymouth for the BBC a few years earlier! I was to appear on the radio programme *Midweek* to talk about the

▶ My demonstration at Waterperry took place in a very large marquee shared with other demonstrators and artists' materials manufacturers. An event of this nature has a very informal atmosphere. Because of this, I find timid students are not afraid to ask questions that they feel would be 'silly' in more formal surroundings

exhibition and was thrilled to be invited to participate. The programme started at 9 a.m. and an hour later June and I were speeding by car towards the Westminster Galleries.

When we arrived, the halls were teaming with people. Members had travelled from Switzerland, Spain, Turkey, Canada, Iceland and even Australia, as well as from all over Britain. In fact, once we got inside, I was so busy talking to people and signing books and catalogues that I didn't move from the same spot for over an hour!

The Right Honourable Peter Brooke MP, then the Secretary of State for National Heritage, had very kindly accepted our invitation to open the first SAA exhibition.

▲ Our trip with students to the Dordogne in 1993 was a great success and June and I enjoyed it very much indeed. Here I am doing a small painting demonstration

What an honour this was! I couldn't help thinking back to the humble origins of Alwyn's Artists! I met the Minister, and June and I showed him around the exhibition, then it was time for his opening speech. Mr Brooke gave a wonderful talk about the amateur painter and the arts in general. While this was happening, I stood on the platform, waiting to give my response. I had never followed a Minister of State before and was feeling very nervous with around fifteen hundred people watching and listening!

When the Minister had finished his speech, I moved to take his place. As the applause died down, I realized I was looking out into a sea of friendly faces. You could feel the excitement – the whole room was buzzing and the atmosphere was electric. I have never felt so exhilarated in front of an audience before. My nerves disappeared – it felt like talking to friends at a party. This was a wonderful feeling and I shall never forget it. I know June felt exactly the same way, too. All the hard work by our dedicated team had been worthwhile, and the first exhibition of the Society of Amateur Artists was a resounding success.

Prior to the exhibition, June and I had been in southern Ireland for three weeks, filming our fifth television series *Crawshaw Paints Acrylics*. June helped me present this series and was featured in each programme painting alongside me. We filmed in County Kerry and the scenery was wonderful but our biggest problem was the weather. At times it

▶ Talking to the Right Honourable Peter Brooke MP in my capacity as President of the Society of Amateur Artists at our first exhibition held in May 1994 at the Westminster Galleries in London

Photographs (above and below): Richard Palmer

◀ This was just a part of the sea of friendly faces I could see when I stood on the stage looking out at the audience at the first SAA exhibition. No wonder I felt at home there! It was wonderful to meet so many members of the society in person

122

was incredibly cold with strong winds and heavy rain. This certainly made filming difficult, but it didn't spoil the beauty of that part of Ireland – or dampen our enthusiasm. When the sun did come out, it was glorious. Back home again, I started writing my usual tie-in book of the television series, and returned to other current projects.

It was at the beginning of this year that June and I decided that we must find a place to escape to every so often, where we could work without too many interruptions. We had done this once before, when we bought our house in Bracklesham Bay in Sussex. Now we were involved in far more than we had ever been before, so it was even more important.

The retreat we found was a small cabin on the Norfolk Broads on the side of the River Thurne and we actually managed to go there on three occasions during 1994. In fact, I wrote some of this book during one stay there and planned our sixth television series, *Crawshaw's Sketching & Drawing Course*, on another visit, as well as doing some painting for pleasure. It was a wonderfully refreshing change and I believe we have now found a good 'safety valve', if we remember to use it properly! Of course, we do find it a little more difficult to 'disappear' now than at Bracklesham Bay twenty years ago. June and I were sitting on the lawn painting during our first visit to our holiday home and a Norfolk wherry (which is similar to a Thames barge)

came sailing slowly past us. Suddenly we heard cries of 'It's Alwyn and June!' from the group of people on board. The wherry moored a few hundred yards upstream at a boatyard and, ten minutes later, we were invaded by half a dozen excited members of the party! Guess what – they were on a painting holiday!

During 1994 June and I started work on a joint book. The main way in which this differs from my other art instruction books is that all the work is done outdoors and any step-by-step stages to paintings are photographed by June or myself as we actually paint them on location. In previous books our 'stage paintings' have usually been done in the studio, working from

Author's collection

◀ **Fig. 116** *The bar at the Blue Bull, Sneem*, 28 x 38 cm (11 x 15 in). I did this painting on television and used brown wrapping paper as my painting surface to demonstrate the versatility of acrylic paint in the series *Crawshaw Paints Acrylics*. While I was being filmed, June sketched some of the people in this typically Irish bar with her 2B pencil (right)

sketches with a photographer standing by to shoot each stage as we paint.

This outdoor method is quite a radical approach. Naturally, the light changes while you are painting outside and photographs can differ in colour appearance. Having to wait for the sun to come out from behind a cloud before you can photograph each stage, as well as working outdoors in all weathers, makes painting a lot more perilous than normal.

So far June and I have had some excellent results and a few disasters! On some occasions we have seriously wondered if it would be better to take the easy way out and work from sketches in the studio. But the idea June and I conceived for this book was to demonstrate how we have exactly the same problems working outdoors as the amateur painter, and to show through painting by stages while on location how to tackle different subjects outdoors. So, wherever we travel at the moment, June and I try to go out and paint for the book, which we have to finish by the end of 1995. This means there's never a dull moment!

People often ask me if my busy way of life ever gets too much for me, and the answer is, 'at times, of course it does'. Whatever job you do there are times when you are overworked and have to call upon your hidden reserves of energy to carry on. But I love painting and enjoy passing my experiences onto others so, while I have those hidden reserves, I will carry on.

▲ **Fig. 117**   Author's collection

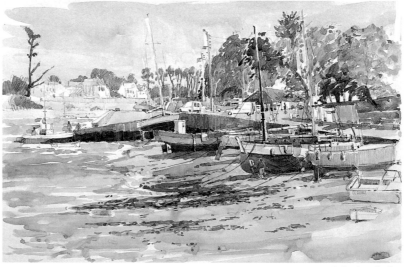

▲ **Fig. 118**   Author's collection

◄ **Figs. 117** and **118** are watercolours, both measuring 28 x 40 cm (11 x 16 in), which I painted when June and I were in Brittany working on our joint book. I did Fig. 117 looking across the estuary towards Benodet. It was a lovely warm day and I was inspired by the activity of the scene. By complete contrast, when I was painting the little harbour across the river from Benodet in Fig 118, I had to stop working on three occasions and protect myself and the painting from sudden heavy showers of rain! But this is something you have to accept when working outdoors, although it doesn't stop you getting very frustrated! In spite of this, I was very happy with the end result

In January of 1995, June and I started to prepare for our sixth television series, *Crawshaw's Sketching & Drawing Course*. The Bahamas Tourist Office had invited us to make the series in their country. This was very exciting, but never having visited the Caribbean before, my immediate thoughts were what was the scenery like for painting and would the hot climate make filming and painting difficult.

Well, we had our usual mix of weather, thunderstorms, rainstorms and gale-force winds but the majority of the days were warm and sundrenched. Some of our painting locations were very uncomfortable because of the heat and humidity but on our very first day of filming in Nassau, at our first location, the weather was perfect, warm and bright. Two young Japanese ladies, an American couple and four English people recognized us, and came up after we had finished filming to ask for autographs. What a wonderful way to start work when you are 8,000 miles from home!

June wasn't feeling so lucky when she filmed in a small covered part of the Straw Market in Nassau which was airless and very warm. She was to draw a woodcarver working and her sketch had to be completed in three minutes. The low ceiling made the atmosphere very claustrophobic and it was also extremely noisy with curious tourists and the excited chatter of the market traders. It took half an hour before we started filming, with a few false starts because of sudden

▲ A moment of concentration in the Straw Market at Nassau during filming for *Crawshaw's Sketching & Drawing Course*

▲ **Fig. 120** June did this delightful pen and watercolour sketch, 17 x 20 cm (7 x 8 in) of a woman working expertly in straw and raffia

▶ **Fig. 119** *Corner of the Straw Market.* Pen and watercolour wash on cartridge paper, 28 x 33 cm (11 x 13 in). I was really inspired by this colourful and lively scene and drew it in pencil first, then painted watercolour freely over the whole painting. When this was dry, I used a fine-line marker to draw in detail

noises or overexcited tourists walking in front of the cameras. June finished her drawing just before she melted away!

One of my worst moments was when I was just starting to sketch a small bell tower in the grounds of St. James Church at Adelaide. June had just been filmed sketching the congregation leaving the church after Sunday service. The crew moved the cameras and got positioned for my sketch.

As I started to talk to the camera, another religious service started in another building nearby and the hallelujahs and loud singing completely drowned our microphone. My adrenalin was at its height at that point, because the lesson I was to teach was perspective and it is not the most relaxing lesson to demonstrate to a televison camera! Having got into the 'dentist's chair', so to speak, filming was cancelled for another day!

Another frustrating artistic moment for me was when we arrived one morning at the harbour in Nassau. I was going to paint a colourful ocean-going tug and had been looking forward to this ever since we had seen it on one of our location-finding days. We had been told that the tug would be there when we came back to film but it had gone! I was terribly disappointed but it was up to me to find another subject to paint so we didn't lose a morning's filming. Eventually I found another tug and enjoyed doing it, but I still think the first one had more character. Oh, well, you can't win 'em all!

◀ **Fig. 121** *Waiting in the Wings*, 38 x 50 cm (15 x 20 in), Waterford 300 lb Rough. This painting and Fig. 82 on page 87 are from a series of watercolours I did for the 1995 Exhibition of the Society of Equestrian Artists, all inspired by a ploughing match I had attended one wet winter's evening. I was thrilled to win the prize again for the Best Watercolour in the Show with this painting

Author's collection

The Bahamian people were very friendly and helpful, making our stay even more memorable in this wonderful part of the world. We were on the islands for four very enjoyable weeks and worked continuously except the last two days which were a holiday. June had planned to go snorkelling while I went deep sea fishing. Sadly, the wind was too strong for either activity.

Back home, we spent the next two months reliving the filming while we wrote the tie-in television book of the series. I had bought a compact disc of local Bahamian music, written by Eddie Minnis, a painter and songwriter we met on Harbour Island. I had this music playing in the background as I wrote the book and it brought memories flooding back.

While we were away, June's first book, *Watercolour Made Easy*, had been published by HarperCollins and work on the television book had to be interrupted by a week's demonstrating and book-signing tour at branches of W H Smith in Croydon, Kingston-upon-Thames and Guildford. This was very exciting and these locations also brought back many early memories for both of us as, when we were first married, we often visited these towns. Of course, they have changed so much in the last thirty years that they are hard to recognize in places. Mind you, so have I – in those days, I had black hair and a black beard! Time changes most things, but June is still as youthful as ever. Lucky me!

Photographs (above and left): Richard Palmer

◀ June and I with Dame Vera Lynn, who kindly opened the 1995 Society of Amateur Artists' Annual Exhibition at the Royal Horticultural Halls ▲ A huge crowd gathered for the official opening ceremony

We had one more major interruption in the April of that year when the Society of Amateur Artists held its Annual Exhibition. This was even bigger than the first one the year before.

Our venue for 1995 was the Royal Horticultural Halls in Westminster, London and the exhibition was opened by Dame Vera Lynn, who has considerable hidden talent as an amateur artist. It was only a few days before the week-long celebrations for the fiftieth anniverary of VE Day and Dame Vera was in great demand for concerts and guest appearances internationally. June and I will always be grateful that she found the time during her busy schedule and for her wonderful support and friendliness on the opening day.

That year 2,756 paintings were hung and 3,000 people attended the opening ceremony. It was a wonderful experience because the paintings on view showed a complete cross-section of amateur work. We also were privileged to have a wall of celebrity amateur artists' paintings this year. Among those exhibited were paintings by Dame Vera Lynn, Sir Harry Secombe, Jan Leeming, Rita Tushingham, the late Arthur English, Catherine Cookson, Richard O'Brien and many others.

It is a wonderful feeling to know that June and I have been instrumental in helping to inspire non-painters to start painting and artists to achieve greater goals. When our television series are being screened we receive more than 100 letters a day. I try to answer these letters personally, either by letter or telephone. This takes a lot of my time but I feel that, kept within reason, it is part of the job I have created.

Often when June and I are in a store or just walking along the street, complete strangers stop us and say, as though we have been friends for years, 'Hello, June and Alwyn. How are you?' The friendliness that has been created by our television series is very satisfying. By complete contrast, a few years ago, I was standing next to someone at a store checkout who was buying some artist materials. He asked the cashier if he had seen 'that artist chap on the TV'. The cashier said that he had and soon they were both deep in conversation about what a good programme it was. I stood next in the queue for five minutes while they discussed me – and they never recognized me!

Because of the commitments and pressures of work during the last ten years, I rarely have time to stand back and reflect on the past and consider the future in an objective way. However, this seems a perfect opportunity to do so.

Looking back, the direction in my working life has changed. June is much more involved and more of our time is now spent teaching through our books, demonstrations, television series, etc. This has given us both a tremendous feeling of fulfilment, especially with the formation of the Society of Amateur Artists. We travel much more now, both in this country and abroad, and have met many wonderful people. We also have the pleasure of making friends with the people who visit our own gallery.

Naturally, there isn't as much time for other activities. I have had fewer 'one-man' exhibitions in the last ten years and have not had any more paintings exhibited at the Royal Society of British Artists since 1986 simply because I have not submitted any.

There have been many personal and family occasions that have been impossible to attend because of pre-booked 'work' engagements. My favourite sport, fishing, has taken a back seat, I have been fishing only a dozen times in the last eight years.

Of course, these changes have also meant that June and I have had a very enjoyable and exciting lifestyle over the past ten years. Occasionally, when work pressure peaks, we do feel that a quiet, boring routine would be very welcome – but only for a couple of days! Perhaps now that our most time-consuming projects are well under way, there may be

▲ This photograph shows June and myself with my sisters Shirley and Pam outside our gallery in Dawlish during a joint exhibition in 1993

more time around the corner to reclaim some of those lost activities.

Many people ask me when am I going to slow down and what my plans are for the future. The answer is simple. While I have good health and enjoy what I do, I will keep going. I only have to think of all the subjects I would like to paint – especially exciting commissions like the tank painting on page 103 – to keep my adrenalin flowing! The thought of just going outdoors and painting still excites me as much as it did during my art school days. I also feel there is still much to be done for the amateur artist through the Society. As I write this, June and I are involved in negotiations for another major joint exhibition and I have still more books in the 'thinking stage', and our seventh television series is being developed.

So the future looks very full and exciting. Who knows, perhaps I may have the privilege of continuing my story in another ten years' time! My sincere thanks go to June and to the many, many friends who have helped me to get this far – of course, not forgetting lady luck!

And a final word for the aspiring artist. My principles for achieving goals as an artist haven't changed in the last ten years but the marketplace has. Because of the recession we have endured in the 1990s, it is much more difficult to sell paintings. Naturally, times will change but, in a climate like this, you must work hard. Remember, it is the will to want to get on that will bring you your rewards.